BEFORE & AFTER
GETTING YOUR
PUPPY

BEFORE & AFTER GETTING YOUR
PUPPY

The Positive Approach to Raising a Happy,
Healthy, & Well-Behaved Dog

DR. IAN DUNBAR

NEW WORLD LIBRARY
NOVATO, CALIFORNIA

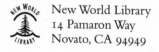

New World Library
14 Pamaron Way
Novato, CA 94949

Before & After Getting Your Puppy combines the books *Before You Get Your Puppy* and *After You Get Your Puppy,* which were originally published in 2001 by James & Kenneth Publishers. These titles remain available in paperback from:

James & Kenneth Publishers
2140 Shattuck Avenue #2406
Berkeley, California 94704
1-800-784-5531
www.jamesandkenneth.com

Cover design by Mary Ann Casler
Interior design and typography by Tona Pearce Myers

Photo Credits: Darlene Bishop, page 14; Kelly Gorman, page 35; Wayne Hightower: pages 26, 27; Carmen Noradunghian, pages 67, 159; Jennifer Bassing, pages 101, 104, 130, 146; Jamie Dunbar, pages 173, 175, 180, 190; Fisher Houtz, page 77; Mimi WheiPing Lou, page 163; Jennifer Messer, pages 192, 193; Sue Pearson, page 78. All other photographs taken by the author.

Library of Congress Cataloging-in-Publication Data
Dunbar, Ian, 1947–
  Before & after getting your puppy : the positive approach to raising a happy, healthy, and well-behaved dog / Ian Dunbar.
      p. cm.
  Includes bibliographical references and index.
  ISBN 1-57731-455-7 (paper over board : alk. paper)
  1. Dogs—Training. 2. Dogs—Behavior. 3. Puppies. 4. Dogs. I. Title: Before and after getting your puppy. II. Title.
  SF431.D77 2004
  636.7'0887—dc22   2004002055

First printing, May 2004
ISBN 1-57731-455-7
Printed in Canada on 100% postconsumer waste recycled paper
Distributed to the trade by Publishers Group West

10   9   8   7   6   5   4   3   2   1

CONTENTS

To all truly exceptional dog breeders, who care as much (if not more) about their dogs' physical and mental health as they do about their dogs' coat color and conformation.

To all knowledgeable veterinarians, who understand the crucially important role of early socialization and training in preventing predictable behavior and temperament problems.

To all caring and responsible puppy owners, who do their very best to choose, raise, and train their puppies to be good-natured and well-mannered companions.

And to all overworked pet dog trainers, shelter staff and volunteers, and animal rescue organizations, who try their best to solve the many problems created by other dog breeders, veterinarians, and dog owners who fail to grasp the big picture.

Acknowledgments

Huge thanks go to Dr. Bruce Boehringer, Jane Stevenson, and Jane's dad for their extremely constructive and critical reviews of my original manuscript, which more than sufficiently pointed out its shortcomings. Thank you all! This book is a complete rewrite. I am especially indebted to Jane for her unwavering enthusiasm and encouragement from the very whelping of this prospective puppy owner education project.

Most of my books are published by James & Kenneth — a small independent "puppy" publisher. Whereas James & Kenneth books are extremely well respected within the dog training profession, they are not well known by the dog-owning public. I am absolutely delighted that such a quality publishing house as New World Library decided to offer this combined hardback edition, which will help spread the word to a much wider audience, thus improving the lives of many more dogs and their owners.

A very, very special thank you to Jason Gardner, my editor at New World, who was the instigator, and has been the driving force, behind this book. Every page has benefited substantially not only from Jason's sharp editing pencil but also from his educated insight into dogs. From the very start of this project, it was obvious to me that Jason must enjoy sharing life with a dog. His many editorial changes champion the viewpoint of dogs and their owners.

Never before has my writing been subjected to such thorough and ruthless editing. The end result, though, is a book devoid of irrelevant material, preachy dogma, and other wooly waffle. Instead it overflows with a wealth of extremely useful and extremely important preventative, how-to, puppy-raising information. Thank you, Bruce. Thank you, Jane. Thank you, Jane's dad. And especially thank you, Jason.

Introduction

Sadly, the majority of puppies fail to live long enough to enjoy their second birthday. They suffer from the terminal illness of being unwanted — failing to live up to the promise and expectation of the Lassie–Benji–Eddie dream. Instead they develop a number of utterly predictable behavior, training, and temperament problems and are surrendered to animal shelters to play lotto with their lives. Many people blame irresponsible ownership for this tragic situation. I would cite lack of know-how. Most prospective puppy owners are simply unaware of the problems that lie ahead; unfortunately, they have little idea how to prevent or resolve them. Ironically, the demise of many dogs stems from novice owners following misleading, erroneous, and in some cases downright bad advice from out-of-date training books.

Dog owners' lack of know-how has to be the responsibility of all doggy professionals, including dog breeders, trainers, veterinarians, animal control officers, and shelter personnel. It is the fault of dog professionals like myself, who have failed to adequately advertise the much easier, quicker, gentler, and altogether more effective and efficient way of raising and training puppies.

In defense of pet professionals like myself, the past two decades have witnessed a revolution in the applied behavioral sciences. Many pet professionals (and hence most dog owners) are simply unaware of the many radical advances in pet dog training and behavior modification.

Only twenty years ago, training was delayed until dogs were six months to a year old, training meant teaching only obedience drills, training was conducted primarily on-leash with repeated leash corrections, behavior modification was largely restricted to punishing dogs for making mistakes, and using food lures and rewards was taboo.

The purpose of this book is to inform pet professionals and prospective and existing puppy owners that puppy training can be quick, easy, and a lot of fun. All serious adult dog behavior, training, and temperament problems can be prevented quite easily with early socialization and lure/reward, puppy-friendly puppy training techniques.

This book will outline common, predictable puppy problems, provide a timetable for puppy development, and suggest a variety of dog-friendly preventative measures and solutions. It emphasizes the overwhelming importance of early socialization, confinement, prevention, and lure/reward training techniques.

Feeling that education can range from boring to hilarious, I have always tried to make my writing enjoyable as well as informative. However, a delicate balance always exists between education and entertainment, so I have also tried to stress the urgency of many of these ideas and drive home the facts that new puppy owners absolutely need to know.

I have also intentionally repeated the most important and pressing points several times throughout the text and in photo captions.

To help new puppy owners get a grasp on all the important information they need to learn, I have outlined six essential developmental deadlines, which form the backbone of this book. But before we explore those deadlines, let's get an overview of what to consider *before* you get your puppy. After introducing these ideas in the first chapter, I'll explore them in detail over the course of the book.

CHAPTER ONE

What's Important to Know Right Away

If you have your heart set on raising and training a puppy, make sure you train yourself beforehand. Remember, it takes only a few days to start ruining an otherwise perfect puppy. Without a doubt, the most important developmental deadline comes before you even think of getting your puppy. It's time to start *your* education about puppy education!

Many first-time puppy owners are surprised when they discover their new companion bites, barks, chews, digs, and marks the house with urine and feces. Yet these are all perfectly normal, natural, and necessary doggy behaviors.

Your canine newcomer is just itching to learn human house manners. It wants to please, but it has to learn how. It's no good keeping house rules a secret. Somebody has to tell the dog. And that somebody is you.

LEARNING THE RULES

Before inviting a puppy to share your life, surely it is only wise and fair to find out beforehand what you might expect from a normal developing puppy, which behaviors and traits you consider unacceptable, and how to modify the pup's inappropriate behavior and temperament accordingly. Specifically, owners need to know how to teach the youngster where to eliminate, what to chew, when to bark, where to dig, to sit when greeting people, to walk calmly on-leash, to settle down and shush when requested, to inhibit its otherwise quite normal biting behavior, and to thoroughly enjoy the company of other dogs and people — especially strangers and children.

PICKING A PUP

Whether selecting your prospective pup from a professional breeder or from a family breeding a litter for the very first time, the criteria are the same. Look for puppies raised indoors around human companionship and influence — specifically around people who have devoted lots of time to the puppies' education.

Your puppy needs to be prepared for the clamor of everyday domestic living — the noise of the vacuum cleaner, pots and pans dropping in the kitchen, football games screaming on the television, children crying, and adults arguing. Exposure to such stimuli while its eyes and ears are still developing allows the puppy (with its blurred vision and muffled hearing) to gradually become accustomed to sights and sounds that might otherwise frighten it when older.

Avoid pups that have been raised in an outdoor run or kennel. Remember, you want a puppy to share your home, so look for a puppy that has been raised in a home. Basement- and kennel-raised puppies are certainly not pet-quality dogs. They are "livestock" on par with veal calves and factory hens. They are neither housetrained nor socialized, and they do not make good companions. Look for litters that have been born and raised in a kitchen or living room.

Choosing a breed is a very personal choice — your choice.

But you will save yourself a lot of unnecessary problems and heartbreak if your choice is an informed and educated one. Choose the breed you like, investigate breed-specific qualities and problems, and then research the best way to raise and train your puppy. Make sure you test-drive several adult dogs of your selected breed or type before you make your final choice. Test-driving adult dogs will quickly teach you everything you need to know about a specific breed. Test-driving adult dogs will also pinpoint gaps in your education about dog behavior and training.

Regardless of your choice, please do not kid yourself that you will get a "perfect" adult dog simply by selecting the "perfect" breed and the "perfect" individual puppy. Any puppy can become a marvelous companion if appropriately socialized and trained. And, no matter what its breed or breeding, any puppy can also become a doggy delinquent if not properly socialized and trained. Please make an intelligent, researched choice when selecting your puppy, but remember: appropriate socialization and training is the single biggest factor determining how closely the dog will approach your view of perfection in adulthood.

No matter your eventual choice, success or failure is entirely in your hands. Your puppy's behavior and temperament now depend completely on good husbandry and training.

LEARNING THE IMPORTANCE OF CONFINEMENT

Your puppy's living quarters need to be designed so that house-training and chewtoy-training are errorless. Each mistake is a potential disaster since it heralds many more to come.

Long-term confinement prevents your puppy from learning to make mistakes around the house, and allows your puppy to teach itself to use an appropriate toilet, to settle down quietly and calmly, and to want to chew appropriate chewtoys. Confinement with chewtoys stuffed with kibble and treats teaches your puppy to enjoy its own company and prepares it for those times when it might be left at home alone.

Short-term close confinement also prevents your puppy from learning to make mistakes around the house, and allows your puppy to teach itself to settle down quietly and calmly, and to want to chew appropriate chewtoys. Additionally, short-term confinement enables you to accurately predict when your puppy needs to relieve itself, so that you may take your puppy to an appropriate toilet area and reward it for using it. The knack of successful housetraining focuses on being able to predict when your puppy "wants to go."

Your puppy's playroom, or long-term confinement area, requires a comfortable bed, a fresh supply of water, a chewtoy, and a toilet.

LEARNING THE IMPORTANCE OF SOCIALIZATION

From the moment you choose your puppy, there is some considerable urgency regarding socialization and training. There is no time to waste. Basically, an adult dog's temperament and behavior habits (both good and bad) are shaped during puppyhood — *very early* puppyhood. In fact, some puppies are well on the road to ruin by the time they are just eight weeks old. It is especially easy to make horrendous mistakes when selecting a pup and during its first few days at home. Such mistakes usually have an indelible effect, influencing your pup's behavior and temperament for the rest of its life. This is not to say that unsocialized and untrained eight-week-old pups cannot be rehabilitated. They can, if you work quickly. But while it's easy to prevent behavior and temperament problems from the beginning, rehabilitation can be both difficult and time-consuming, and it is unlikely that your pup will ever become the adult dog he could have been.

THE SERIOUSNESS OF SIMPLE BEHAVIOR PROBLEMS

Learn how to make intelligent choices when selecting your pup. Learn how to implement a course of errorless housetraining and errorless chewtoy-training the moment your puppy arrives at its new home. Any housesoiling or chewing mistake you allow

My friend Nancy's house after a shepherd party! Chewtoys stuffed with food would have provided the dogs with appropriate amusement and occupational therapy to pass the time when left alone.

your puppy to make is absolute silliness and absolute seriousness: silliness because you are creating lots of future headaches for yourself, and seriousness because millions of dogs are euthanized each year simply because their owners did not know how to housetrain or chewtoy-train them.

If your pup is ever left unsupervised indoors it will most certainly chew household articles and soil your house. Although these teeny accidents do little damage in themselves, they set the precedent for your puppy's choice of toys and toilets for many months to come.

Allowing a single housesoiling mistake is a disaster since it sets the precedent for your puppy's toilet area and signals many more mistakes to come.

You should treat any puppy housesoiling or house-destruction mistake as a potential disaster, since it predicts numerous future mistakes from a dog with larger bladder and bowels and much more destructive jaws. Many owners begin to notice their puppy's destructiveness by the time it is four to five months old, when the pup is characteristically relegated outdoors. Natural inquisitiveness prompts the lonely pup to dig, bark, and escape in its quest for some form of occupational therapy to pass the day in solitary confinement. Once the neighbors complain about the dog's incessant barking and periodic escapes, the dog is often further confined to a garage or basement. Usually though, this is only a temporary measure until the dog is surrendered to a local animal

Digging, barking, and escaping are usually the secondary problems of unhousetrained adolescent dogs that have been relegated to a life of solitary confinement and boredom in the yard. Housetrain your dog, and then you may leave him indoors. Magically, the digging and escaping problems will disappear.

One of the best ways to reduce excessive barking is to teach your puppy to speak on cue. Training your pup to bark on request facilitates teaching him to shush on request, since you may now shush-train the pup both at your convenience and when he is calm and focused. Instead of trying to quiet your puppy when he is excitedly barking, request that your pup bark and then shush when he is calm.

shelter to play the lotto of life. Fewer than 25 percent of surrendered dogs are adopted, of which about half are returned as soon as the new owners discover their adopted adolescent's annoying problems.

The above summarizes the fate of many dogs. This is especially sad because all these simple problems could be prevented so easily. Housetraining and chewtoy-training are hardly rocket science. But you do need to know what to do. And you need to know what to do before you bring your puppy home.

CHAPTER TWO

The Developmental Deadlines

As soon as your puppy comes home, the clock is running. Within just three months, your puppy will need to meet six crucial developmental deadlines. If your puppy fails to meet any of these deadlines, it is unlikely to achieve its full potential. In terms of your dog's behavior and temperament, you will probably be playing catch-up for the rest of your dog's life. Most important of all, you simply cannot afford to neglect the socialization and bite inhibition deadlines.

1. Your Doggy Education (before searching)

2. Evaluating Puppy's Progress (before selection)

3. Errorless Housetraining and Chewtoy-Training (the day your puppy comes home)

4. Socialization with People (by twelve weeks of age)

5. Learning Bite Inhibition (by eighteen weeks of age)

6. The World at Large (by five months of age and there-after)

If you already have a puppy and feel that you are behind, do not throw in the towel. You must acknowledge, however, that you are well behind and that your puppy's socialization and education are now a dire emergency. Immediately do your best to catch up. Contact a pet dog trainer immediately. To locate a trainer in your area, call 1-800-PET-DOGS for the Association of Pet Dog Trainers. Invite family, friends, and neighbors to help you with your puppy's remedial socialization and training. Maybe take a week or two off of work to devote to your puppy. The younger your puppy, the easier and quicker it is to catch up on her developmental timetable and minimize losses. Every day you delay, however, makes it harder.

1. YOUR DOGGY EDUCATION

Planning for a new puppy begins with the owner's education about puppy education.

Before you search for your puppy, you need to know what sort of dog to look for, where to get it, and when to get it. An educated choice is generally far better than an impulsive puppy purchase. Additionally, you need to thoroughly familiarize yourself with the developmental deadlines; they become urgent and crucial the day you select your puppy. Take your time to review this book and then make a thoughtful choice because your dog's future depends on it.

2. EVALUATING PUPPY'S PROGRESS

Before you select your puppy (usually at eight weeks of age), you need to know how to select a good breeder and how to select a good puppy. Specifically, you need to know how to assess your puppy's behavioral development. By eight weeks of age: your puppy must have become thoroughly accustomed to a home physical environment, especially to all sorts of potentially scary noises; your puppy should already have been handled by many people, especially men and children; your puppy's errorless housetraining and chewtoy-training should be under way; and your puppy should already have a rudimentary understanding of basic manners. Your puppy should come, sit, lie down, and rollover when requested. In other words, in preparation for household living, the litter of

This candidate for Rocky Mountain Search and Rescue was carefully selected at eight weeks of age from an already carefully selected litter.

puppies must have been raised indoors and around people and not in some secluded backyard or kennel.

3. ERRORLESS HOUSETRAINING AND CHEWTOY-TRAINING

You need to institute an errorless housetraining and chewtoy-training program the very first day your puppy comes home. This is so important during the first week, when puppies characteristically learn good or bad habits that set the precedent for weeks, months, and sometimes years to come.

Be absolutely certain that you fully understand the principles of long-term and short-term confinement before you bring your new puppy home. With a long-term and short-term confinement schedule, housetraining and chewtoy-training are easy, efficient, and errorless. During her first few weeks at home, regular confinement (with chewtoys stuffed with kibble) teaches the puppy to teach herself to chew chewtoys, to settle down calmly and quietly, and not to become a recreational barker. Moreover, short-term confinement allows you to predict when your puppy needs to relieve herself, so that you may take her to the right spot and reward her for eliminating.

4. SOCIALIZATION WITH PEOPLE

The Critical Period of Socialization ends by three months of age! This is the crucial developmental stage during which puppies learn to accept and enjoy the company of other dogs and people. Thus your puppy needs to be socialized to people by the time he is twelve weeks old, making this a most *urgent* deadline. However, since his series of puppy immunization injections is incomplete at this point, a young pup needs to meet people in the safety of his own home. As a rule of thumb, your puppy needs to meet at least a hundred different people during his first month at home. Not only is this easier to do than it might sound, it's also lots of fun.

Puppies must be socialized to people, especially men and children, before they are three months old.

5. LEARNING BITE INHIBITION

Bite inhibition is the single most important lesson a dog must learn. Adult dogs have teeth and jaws that can hurt and harm. All animals must learn to inhibit use of their weapons against their own kind, but domestic animals must learn to be gentle with all animals, especially people. Domestic dogs must learn to inhibit their biting toward all animals, especially toward other dogs and people. The narrow time window for developing a "soft mouth" begins to close at four and a half months of age, about the time when the adult canine teeth first show. Providing your puppy with an ideal forum to learn bite inhibition is the most pressing reason to enroll her in puppy classes before she is eighteen weeks old.

Bite inhibition is all-important. Puppies must learn to inhibit the force of their biting before they are taught to stop biting and mouthing altogether.

6. THE WORLD AT LARGE

To ensure that your well-rounded and well-schooled puppy remains a mannerly, well-socialized, and friendly dog throughout adulthood, your dog needs to meet *unfamiliar* people and *unfamiliar* dogs on a regular basis. In other words, your dog needs to be walked at least once a day. Your puppy may be taken for rides in the car and to visit friends' houses as early as you like. Start walking your puppy as soon as your veterinarian says it's safe to do so.

Maintaining socialization requires ongoing socialization throughout puppyhood, adolescence, and adulthood. Your dog will continue to gain confidence with continued exposure to unfamiliar people, unfamiliar dogs, and unfamiliar situations.

My goal with these deadlines isn't to scare you into thinking that puppy ownership is all work and no fun. It's certainly a lot of work, but it's mostly fun! I've designed these deadlines — based on years of canine behavior research — to take the guesswork out of raising a happy, healthy puppy. The real fun comes when you get to enjoy living with a well-mannered, friendly, lovely, and lovable adult dog.

Your life is about to change. You are about to enjoy all the joys of dog ownership — long, energetic, or relaxing walks, trips in the car, afternoons in the dog park, picnics on the beach, plus so many enjoyable organized doggy activities. With the deadlines firmly in mind, and the techniques outlined here in your puppy-training arsenal, you and your puppy will enjoy a long, happy life together.

A Rolls Royce doggy personality requires a Rolls Royce owner education.

CHAPTER THREE

THE FIRST DEVELOPMENTAL DEADLINE

Your Doggy Education
(Before You Search for Your Puppy)

Amost important developmental deadline comes before you even begin your search for a puppy: namely, your education about puppy education. Just as you would learn how to drive before setting off in a car, you should learn how to raise and train a puppy *before* you get one.

Some owners want heaven and earth from their pups; others only demand magic and miracles. Owners want the puppy to be perfectly well-behaved and to amuse itself when left at home alone for hours on end. And they assume the pup will magically grow up to act this way without guidance.

It is simply not fair to keep house rules a secret from your puppy, only to moan and groan when it predictably finds doggy ways to entertain himself and break rules he didn't even know existed. If you have house rules, somebody needs to teach them to the puppy. And that somebody is you.

Luckily, dogs have their natural activity peaks at dawn and dusk, so many are quite happy to settle down and snooze the day away. However, some dogs are not. Some dogs are simply more active than others, and when left at home alone become exceedingly stressed and may destroy the house and garden in the space of a day.

Puppy owners are often surprised when their new puppy bites, barks, chews, digs, and decorates the floors with urine and feces. Yet this is what dogs do. How did you expect your dog to speak? To moo? To meow? And what did you expect your dog to do to pass the time of day? Housework? To mop and clean floors and dust the furniture? Or to amuse herself reading books, watching television, or doing macramé?

Many owners appear to be at a further loss when confronted by utterly predictable problems, such as jumping up, pulling on-leash, and expressing the boundless energy and exuberance accompanying doggy adolescence. Additionally, owners are incredulous if their adolescent or adult dog bites or fights. When dogs are

undersocialized, harassed, abused, frightened, or otherwise upset, what do we expect them to do? Call a lawyer? Of course they bite! Biting is as normal an ingredient of canine behavior as wagging the tail or burying a bone.

Dogs are dogs. Not surprisingly, puppies behave like dogs: they chew, dig, bark, communicate largely via body language and p-mail, and spend much of their free time sniffing rear ends.

Before inviting a puppy to share your life, surely it is only wise and fair to find out beforehand what you might expect from a normal developing puppy, which behaviors and traits you might consider unacceptable, and how to modify the pup's inappropriate behavior and temperament accordingly. Specifically, owners need to know how to teach the youngster when to bark, what to chew, where to dig, where to perform its toilet duties, to sit when greeting people, to walk calmly on-leash, to settle down and shush when requested, to inhibit its otherwise normal biting behavior, and to thoroughly enjoy the company of other dogs and of people, especially men, strangers, and children.

It is vital that you know what and how to teach your puppy, before you get her. So in addition to this book, read other books, watch videos, observe puppy-training classes, and above all, test-drive as many adult dogs as possible. Talk to owners at puppy class and discover what types of problems they are experiencing. New puppy owners are ruthlessly honest when describing their puppy's problems.

WHICH TYPE OF DOG?

There are many things to consider when choosing a puppy, including which breed or type, and the optimal age of acquisition. Obviously, you want to choose a dog who is best suited to you and your lifestyle. Rather than offering specific recommendations, I will list some of the more important guidelines.

First, please do not kid yourself that all you have to do is select the "perfect" breed and the "perfect" individual puppy and it will automatically grow up into the "perfect" adult dog. I must re-emphasize: any puppy can become a marvelous companion if appropriately socialized and trained. And, no matter what its breed or breeding, any puppy can become a doggy delinquent if not properly socialized and trained. Please make an intelligent, researched choice when selecting your puppy, but remember: appropriate socialization and training is the single biggest factor determining how closely the dog will approach your view of perfection in adulthood.

Second, seek advice from the best sources. Common mistakes are to take breed advice from veterinarians, health advice from breeders, and all-important behavior and training advice from veterinarians, breeders, and pet-store personnel. The best plan is to seek training and behavior advice from trainers and behavior counselors, health advice from veterinarians, breed advice from breeders, and product advice from pet-store personnel. And if you really want to know what's going on, check out a local puppy class and chat with the owners; they'll give you the cold, hard facts regarding what it's really like to live with a puppy.

Third, evaluate all advice carefully. Apply the common sense principle: does it make sense to you? Is the advice relevant to your family and your lifestyle? Whereas most advice is sound, some can be irrelevant, hypocritical, preachy, or questionable. And occasionally, "advice" can be just downright bad.

Example 1: One breeder told a couple they could not buy a puppy unless they had a fenced yard and one of them was home all day. Yet the breeder herself had no fenced yard and her twenty or so dogs lived in crates in a kennel a good forty yards away from her house and any hope of human companionship. Duh!??

Example 2: Many people are advised not to get a large dog if they live in an apartment. On the contrary! As long as they receive regular walks, large dogs make wonderful apartment companions. Compared with smaller dogs, large dogs often settle down quicker and bark less. Many little dogs exasperate owners and neighbors by being active and noisy, and running amuck. Smaller dogs make wonderful apartment companions, however, so long as they are trained to settle down and shush.

Example 3: Many veterinarians advise that golden retrievers and Labrador retrievers are the best dogs with children. *All* breeds of dog can make good companions for children, provided that they have been trained how to act around children, and provided that the children have been taught how to act around dogs! Otherwise, dogs — including Goldens and Labs — are likely to be frightened and irritated by children, or excited and incited by their antics.

Remember, you are selecting a puppy to live with you for a good long time. Choosing a puppy to share your life is a very personal choice — your choice. You will save yourself a lot of unnecessary problems and heartbreak if your choice is an informed and educated one.

In reality, though, people seldom pay heed to well-meaning advice and usually end up choosing with heart instead of head. Indeed many people end up choosing a dog along the same lines as they might choose a lifelong human companion: based on coat color, conformation, and cuteness. But regardless of the many reasons for selecting a particular puppy — whether pedigree, conformation, cuteness, or general health — the success of the endeavor ultimately depends almost entirely on the pup's education regarding appropriate behavior and training.

MIXED BREED OR PURE BREED?

Again, this decision is a personal choice that only you can make. The most obvious difference is that pure breeds are more predictable in terms of looks and behavior, whereas each mixed breed is utterly unique — one of a kind.

Regardless of your personal preference for attractiveness, attentiveness, and activity, you would do well to consider general health and life expectancy. By and large, due to lack of inbreeding, mixed breeds are healthier genetic stock; they tend to live longer and have fewer health problems. On the other hand, at a pure-breed kennel, it is possible to check out the friendliness, basic manners, general health, and life expectancy of several generations of your prospective puppy's forebears.

WHICH BREED?

I am strongly opposed to suggesting breeds for people. Recommending specific breeds may sound like helpful and harmless advice, but it is insidiously dangerous and not in the best interests of dogs or of dog-owning families. Advice either for or against specific breeds often leads owners to believe that training is either unnecessary or impossible. Thus many poor dogs grow up without an education.

Also, when certain breeds are recommended, other breeds are automatically being advised against. "Experts" often suggest that certain breeds are too big, too small, too active, too lethargic, too fast, too slow, too smart, or too dumb, and therefore too difficult to train. Well, we know that regardless of helpful advice, people are probably going to pick the breed they wanted in the first place. But now they may feel disinclined to train the puppy, feeling that the process is going to be difficult and time-consuming. Furthermore, owners may rationalize their negligence by citing one of the convenient excuses listed above.

Breed is a very personal choice. Choose the breed you like, investigate breed-specific qualities and problems, and then research the best way to raise and train your pup. If you select what others consider an easy breed to raise and train, train him so that he becomes the very best individual — an ambassador — of that breed. And if you select a breed that some people consider difficult to raise and train, train him, train him, and train him, so that he becomes the very best example — an ambassador — of the breed.

Regardless of your eventual choice, and certainly once you have made it, success or failure is now entirely in your hands. Your puppy's behavior and temperament now depend completely on good husbandry and training.

When evaluating different breeds, the good points are obvious. What you need to find out are the breed's bad points. You need to investigate potential breed-specific (or line-specific) problems and to know how to deal with them. If you want to find out more about a specific breed, find at least six adult dogs of the breed you have selected. Talk to their owners at length, but most importantly, meet the dogs! Examine and handle them; play with them and work them. See if the dogs welcome being petted by a stranger — you. Will they sit? Do they walk nicely on-leash? Are they quiet or noisy? Are they calm and collected, or are they hyperactive and rambunctious? Can you examine their ears, eyes, paws, and rear end? Can you open their muzzle? Can you get them to roll over? Are the owners' houses and gardens still in

good condition? And most important, do the dogs like people and other dogs?

Learn what to expect, because when your eight-week-old puppy comes home it will grow up with frightening speed. In just four months' time your pup will develop into a six-month-old adolescent that has gained almost adult size, strength, and speed, while at the same time retaining many puppy constraints on learning. Your puppy has so much to learn before he collides with impending adolescence.

In terms of personality, behavior, and temperament, please be aware that dogs of the same breed may show considerable variation. If you have siblings or more than one child you probably appreciate the incredible range of temperaments and personalities of children from the same parents. Dogs are similar. Indeed, there may be as much variation of behavior among individuals of the same litter as there is among dogs of different breeds.

Environmental influences (socialization and training) exert a

Basic handling exercises are the most important aspect of "test-driving" different dogs. Make sure each dog enjoys being gently restrained (snuggled, cuddled, and hugged) as you examine his ears, muzzle, and paws.

far greater impact on desired domestic behavior and temperament than genetic heredity. For example, the temperamental differences between a good (educated) malamute and a bad (uneducated) malamute or between a good golden retriever and a bad golden retriever are much greater than temperamental differences between a golden and a malamute with an equivalent experiential and educational history. A dog's education is always the biggest factor determining its future behavior and temperament.

Please make sure you fully understand the above paragraph. I am not saying training necessarily has a greater effect on dog behavior than genetic heredity. Rather, I am stating quite categorically that attaining a desired domestic dog behavior is almost entirely dependent on socialization and training. For example, dogs bark, bite, urine mark, and wag their tails largely for genetic reasons — because they are dogs. The frequency of their barks, however, the severity of their bites, the location of their urine marks, and the enthusiasm of their tail wags depend pretty much on the nature of their socialization and training. Your dog's domestic success is in your hands.

The author with DogStar Moose and trainer Mathilde DeCagny at the Association of Pet Dog Trainers' conference in San Diego.

MOVIE DOGSTARS

When selecting a breed, don't be duped by celebrity dogs appearing in films or on television. These dogs are highly trained actors. In fact, Lassie has been played by at least eight different dogs. The dogs are acting, and often the requirements of their role mask their true breed and individual characteristics. This is no different from Anthony Hopkins playing Hannibal Lecter in *The Silence of the Lambs* and C. S. Lewis in *Shadowlands* — two very different roles, and both of them completely different from what we

may suppose is the real Anthony Hopkins. It's acting, and in a sense *you* need to teach your puppy how to act — that is, how to act appropriately in a variety of domestic settings, such as the living room and the park.

Eddie (Moose) appears to be calm and controlled on the set of *Frasier,* because Moose The Active was trained to be calm and controlled to play the role of Eddie. Moreover, Eddie's endearing television demeanor and his acquired social savvy, charming manners, and acting skills have successfully overcome his original delinquent disposition.

An excerpt from "Doggy Dialogues" — an interview between yours truly, Moose, and his trainer, Mathilde DeCagny — follows.

IAN DUNBAR: What is Moose really like?

MATHILDE DECAGNY: Moose has his own personality! I got him when he was about two years old and he was a terror — a tyrant — selfish and mischievous with lots of negativity. He'd constantly try to escape, he'd chase squirrels, he'd get into trash and into dogfights. His recall was non-existent. I could never get him to come back to me. And I wasn't the first one who had tried. He would pee everywhere and he was just very, very...

IAN DUNBAR: He sounds like a normal human movie star.

MATHILDE DECAGNY: Absolutely! But he's changed so much. He's a different dog. He's interested in training and he loves the idea of being busy. He has always been impatient — no patience whatsoever. It was always Moose, Moose, Moose — right now, right now. So through the years I've taught him to be more patient and to be a little nicer with me. Originally he was extremely independent and didn't care about being petted. He had owners before me who just couldn't cope with him because there was no giving on his end. Now he's very affectionate.

(Excerpt from "Doggy Dialogues" reprinted from the magazine *The Bark* with permission of the publishers.)

WHEN TO GET A PUPPY

Aside from the obvious answer — not before you are ready — the time to get a dog is when you have completed your doggy education. And when the pup is ready.

An important consideration is the age of the pup. Most puppies change homes at some time in their life, usually from the home where they were born to the homes of their new human companions. The optimal time for a puppy to change homes depends on many variables, including his emotional needs, his all-important socialization schedule, and the level of doggy expertise in each household.

Leaving home can be traumatic, and limiting the pup's emotional trauma is a prime consideration. If the puppy leaves home too early, he will miss out on early pup-pup and pup-mother interactions. And since the first weeks in a new home are often spent in a doggy social vacuum, the developing puppy may grow up undersocialized toward his own kind. On the other hand, the longer the puppy stays in his original home the more attached he becomes to its doggy family and the harder the eventual transition. A delayed transition also postpones all-important socialization with the new family.

Eight weeks of age has long been accepted as the optimal time to acquire a new pup. By eight weeks, sufficient dog-dog socialization has taken place with mother and littermates to tide the puppy over until he is old enough to safely meet and play with other dogs in puppy class and dog parks. Yet the puppy is still young enough to form a strong bond with the members of his new family.

The relative level of doggy expertise in each home is a vital consideration in determining whether the puppy is better off staying longer in his original home or leaving earlier to live with his new owners. It is often assumed that breeders are experts and owners are rank novices, so that it makes sense to leave the pup with the breeder as long as possible. A conscientious breeder is usually better qualified to socialize, housetrain, and chewtoy-train the puppy. When this is true, it makes sense to get the puppy when he is older. (In fact, I often ask novice owners whether they have considered a socially mature and well-trained adult dog as an alternative to a young pup.)

This of course presupposes the breeder's superior expertise. Unfortunately, just as there are excellent, average, novice, and irresponsible owners, there are also excellent, average, novice, and irresponsible breeders. With the combination of an experienced owner and a less-than-average breeder, the puppy would be better off moving to his new home as early as possible, certainly by six to eight weeks at the latest. If you feel you are a qualified puppy raiser but the breeder will not let you take your pup home before eight weeks of age, look elsewhere. Remember, you are searching for a puppy to live with you, not with the breeder. In fact, you might be better off looking elsewhere anyway, since a less-than-average breeder probably produces less-than-average puppies.

Adopting an adult dog from an animal shelter or rescue organization can be a marvelous alternative to raising a puppy. Some shelter and rescue dogs are well trained and simply need a home. Others have a few behavior problems and require remedial education. Some dogs are purebred; most are mixed breeds. The key to finding a good shelter or rescue dog is selection, selection, selection! Take plenty of time to test-drive each prospective candidate. Each dog is unique.

WHERE TO GET A PUPPY

Whether selecting your prospective pup from a professional breeder or from a family breeding a litter for the very first time, the criteria are the same. First, look for puppies raised indoors around human companionship and influence. Avoid pups raised in an outdoor run or kennel. Remember, you want a puppy to share your home, and so look for a puppy that has been raised in a home. Second, assess your prospective puppy's current socialization and education status. Regardless of breed, breeding, pedigree, and lineage, if your prospective puppy's socialization and training programs are not well under way by eight weeks of age, he is already developmentally retarded.

HOW TO SELECT A GOOD BREEDER

A good breeder will be extremely choosy in accepting prospective puppy buyers. A prospective owner should be equally choosy when selecting a breeder. A prospective owner can begin to evaluate a breeder's expertise by noting whether she ranks the puppies' mental well-being and physical health above their good looks. Assess several factors: whether the breeder's adult dogs are all people-friendly and well trained; whether your prospective puppy's parents, grandparents, great-grandparents, and other relations live to a ripe old age; and whether your prospective pup is already well-socialized and well-trained.

Friendly dogs are self-apparent when you meet them, and so meet as many of your prospective puppy's relatives as possible. Friendly dogs are living proof of good socialization by a good breeder.

Beware the breeder who is only willing to show you puppies. First, a good breeder will take the time to see how you get along with adult dogs before letting you anywhere near the pups. A good breeder wouldn't let you leave with a puppy if you didn't know how to handle an adult dog, which your puppy will be in just a few months. Second, you want to evaluate as many adult dogs as possible from your prospective puppy's family and line before you let a litter of supercute puppies steal your heart. If all the adult dogs are people-friendly and well-behaved, it is a good bet that you have discovered an exceptional breeder.

Your ultimate evaluation of a breeder centers on the behavior and temperament of his or her puppies as well as their estimated life expectancy. (See the Second Developmental Deadline.) Similarly, the search for a good puppy depends on finding a good breeder. The puppies' physique, behavior, and temperament all reflect the breeder's expertise. Thus, searching for a good breeder and selecting a quality puppy pretty much go hand in hand.

The single best indicator of general health, good behavior, and temperament is the overall life expectancy of a kennel line. Check to see that your prospective puppy's parents, grandparents, great-grandparents, and other relations are still alive and healthy or that they died at a ripe old age. Conscientious breeders will have telephone numbers readily available of previous puppy buyers and of the breeders of the other dogs in your prospective puppy's pedigree. If the breeder is not eager to share information regarding life expectancy and the incidence of breed-specific diseases, look elsewhere. You will eventually find a breeder who will accommodate your concerns. Before you open your heart to a young pup, you certainly want to maximize the likelihood that the two of you will be spending a long and healthy life together. Additionally, long-lived dogs advertise good temperament and training, since dogs with behavior and temperament problems generally have short life expectancies.

PUPPY VS. ADULT

Before rushing ahead and getting a puppy, it's a good idea to at least consider the pros and cons of adopting an adult dog. Certainly, there are several advantages to getting a pup, the foremost being that you may mold the puppy's behavior and temperament to suit your own particular lifestyle. This, of course, presumes you know how to train and have the time to do it. Sometimes you might not. And so in a lot of ways an adolescent or adult dog with a Kennel Club obedience title and a Canine Good Citizen Test may make a more suitable companion — especially for a two-income family whose members barely have the time to get together as a family themselves.

Little brown dog Oliver (adopted from the Chicago Heights Humane Society at nine months of age) has now graduated to NPD (Near Perfect Dog) status.

Additionally, a two-year-old (or older) adult dog's habits, manners, and temperament are already well established, for better or for worse. Traits and habits may change over time, but compared with the behavioral flexibility of young puppies, an older dog's good habits are as resistant to change as their bad habits. Consequently, it is possible to test-drive a number of adult shelter dogs and select one free of problems and with an established personality to your liking. Please at least consider this alternative.

If you still have your heart set on raising and training a puppy, do make sure you educate yourself beforehand. Only search for a puppy after you have learned how to raise and train one. Remember, it takes only a few days' start to ruin an otherwise perfect puppy.

Whether you decide to get a puppy or adopt an adult dog, please make an appointment with your veterinarian to get your puppy or dog neutered. There are simply too many unwanted dogs. Millions are euthanized each year. Please don't add to the numbers.

"Ratweiler" Tater Tot (adopted at two years of age) was awarded First Place in the KPIX Late Show Stupid Pet Tricks competition and has won the K9 Games® Waltzes with Dogs competition twice.

Grizzly old Ashby (saved from the syringe at ten years of age) lived out his sunset years in some considerable comfort at Villa Phoenix.

Big red Claude (recently adopted at one year of age from the San Francisco SPCA) is still a bit of a project. But he sits beautifully for lettuce!

SHOPPING LIST

Once you have completed your doggy education it is time to shop for your prospective puppy. Many training books, pet stores, and dog catalogs display an awesome and confusing array of doggy products and training equipment. Many products are completely unnecessary, whereas others are essential. Consequently, I have listed the essentials with personal preferences in parentheses.

1. Dog crate, and maybe an exercise pen or baby gate barrier

2. At least six chewtoys to stuff with kibble and treats (Kong products and bones are excellent)

3. Doggy toilet (Construct your own. See p. 63.)

4. Water bowl

5. Dog food (dry kibble) Note: During her first few weeks at home, make sure your puppy receives all food stuffed in chewtoys, or handfed as rewards for socialization and training. Buy your puppy a food bowl once she is socialized, well-trained, and has impeccable household manners

6. Freeze-dried liver for men, strangers, and children to win your puppy's confidence and as rewards for house-training

7. Martingale collar, leash, and maybe a Gentle Leader (made by Premier Pet Products), a uniquely designed head halter to prevent the dog from pulling by leading him by the nose rather than the collar

Most of the above items, plus informative books and videos (pp. 213–216), are available from your local pet store, or mail order and online from Best Dog Stuff at: 1-800-297-0225 or www.bestdogstuff.com.

CHAPTER FOUR

THE SECOND DEVELOPMENTAL DEADLINE

Evaluating Puppy's Progress

(Before You Select Your Puppy)

B y the time you bring your new puppy home, say at eight weeks of age, he should already be accustomed to an indoor domestic environment (especially one with noises) and well-socialized with people. Similarly, housetraining, chewtoy-training, and tutoring in basic manners should be well under way. If not, your prospective puppy's social and mental development are already way behind schedule and will require your prompt and full attention. Otherwise you will be playing behavioral catch-up for the rest of your dog's life. Certainly it is possible to bring an eight-week-old puppy up to speed, but it will take an immediate and intensive effort on your part. Moreover, the potential success of rehabilitation worsens with every day you let slip by.

Make absolutely certain your prospective puppy has been raised indoors in close contact with people who have devoted lots of time to its education.

If a dog is expected to live in a household with people, obviously it needs to have been raised in a household with people. Your puppy needs to be prepared for the clamor of everyday domestic living: the noise of the vacuum cleaner, doors slamming, loud music, children shouting and playing. Exposure to such stimuli while its eyes and ears are still developing allows the puppy (with its limited vision and hearing) to gradually become accustomed to sights and sounds that might otherwise startle it when older.

There is not much point in choosing a puppy that has been raised in the relative social isolation of a backyard, basement, barn, garage, or kennel, where there is precious little opportunity for interaction with people and where a puppy has become accustomed to soiling his living area and yapping a lot. Puppies raised in physical seclusion and partial social isolation are hardly prepared for household living, and they are certainly not prepared for encounters with children or men. Backyard- and kennel-raised puppies are certainly not pet-quality dogs; they are livestock. Look elsewhere! Look for litters born and raised in a kitchen or living room.

If you want a companion dog to share your home, obviously he should have been raised in a home, not a cage.

HOW TO SELECT A GOOD PUPPY

Your prospective puppy should feel thoroughly at ease being handled by strangers — you and your family. The puppy should be fully desensitized to sounds before he is four weeks old. Likewise, his housetraining program should be well under way, his favorite toy should be a chewtoy (stuffed with puppy chow), and he should happily and eagerly come, follow, sit, lie down, and roll over when requested. If these are not so, either your puppy is a slow learner or he has had a poor teacher. In either case, look elsewhere.

An essential ingredient of puppy husbandry is regular (several times a day) handling, gentling, and calming by a wide variety of people, especially children, men, and strangers. These exercises are especially important during the early weeks and especially with those breeds that are notoriously tricky when handled by strangers — that is, several Asian breeds, plus many herding, working, and terrier breeds — in other words, most breeds of dog!

The second most important quality in any dog is that he enjoys interacting with people, specifically that he enjoys being handled by all people, especially children, men, and strangers. Early socialization easily prevents serious adult problems. (A reminder: the single most important quality for a dog is developing bite inhibition and a soft mouth during puppyhood.)

HANDLING AND GENTLING

If you want a cuddly adult dog, she needs to have been cuddled regularly as a puppy. Certainly, neonatal pups are pretty fragile and helpless critters; they can barely walk and they have a number of sensory constraints. But they still need to be socialized. Neonatal pups are extremely sensitive and impressionable, and this is the very best time to accustom them to being handled. Neonatal puppies may not see or hear very well, but they can smell and feel. Of course, neonatal and early puppy socialization, being of paramount importance, must be done gently and carefully.

- Ask the breeder how many people have handled, gentled, trained, and played with the pups daily.

- Specifically, ask the breeder how many children, men, and strangers have worked with the puppies.

- Handle each puppy to see how she enjoys being cuddled (gently restrained); specifically, see how she enjoys being stroked and massaged (examined) around her neck, muzzle, ears, paws, and rear end.

ALPHA ROLLOVERS???

The Trainers from the Dark Side suggest grabbing a young pup by the cheeks, flipping him onto his back, and forcibly holding him down to see if he struggles. They call this procedure the Alpha Rollover. It is as stupid as it is cruel. How would you feel if a dog weighing two thousand pounds unexpectedly grabbed you by the scruff and stared menacingly into your eyes? If you didn't struggle, you would most probably go limp out of fear and wet your pants. All this silly maneuver proves is that puppies are scared when people frighten them and that, of course, scared puppies either struggle or go limp.

Certainly you need to determine how readily your potential pup accepts and enjoys handling and restraint, but it is not necessary to frighten the living daylights out of him. Simply pick up the puppy and gently cuddle him in your arms. You'll soon find out whether he relaxes like a rag doll or kicks and struggles. If he struggles, hold on gently while you soothingly stroke him between the eyes or massage his ears or chest, and see how quickly you can calm him down.

SOUND SENSITIVITY

Exposure to a variety of sounds should commence well before the eyes and ears are fully opened, especially with sound-sensitive dogs, such as herding and obedience breeds.

It is quite normal for puppies to react to noises. What you are trying to evaluate is the extent of each pup's reaction and the pup's bounce-back time. For example, we expect a puppy to react to a sudden and unexpected loud noise, but we do not expect him to go to pieces. Judge whether the puppy reacts or overreacts to sounds and time how long it takes for the puppy to approach and take a food treat (the bounce-back time). Expect immeasurably short bounce-back times from bull breeds, and short bounce-backs from working dogs and terriers, but be prepared for longer bounce-back times from toys and herding breeds. Regardless of a dog's breed or type, however, excessive overreaction, panic, or extremely lengthy bounce-back times are all proof of insufficient socialization. Unless successfully rehabilitated, such pups may become extremely reactive and difficult to live with when they grow up.

- Ask the breeder about the extent of the litter's exposure to domestic noise. Are the puppies being raised indoors?

- Specifically, ask the breeder whether or not the puppies have been exposed to loud and unexpected noises, such as adults shouting, children crying, television (male voices shouting and screaming on ESPN), radio, and music (country, rock, and classical — maybe Tchaikovsky's *1812 Overture*).

- Evaluate the puppies' response to a variety of noises: people talking, laughing, crying, and shouting, a whistle, a hiss, or a single hand clap.

HOUSEHOLD ETIQUETTE

Ask the breeder about the litter's ongoing errorless housetraining and chewtoy-training program. Try to observe the litter for at least two hours and pay attention to what each puppy chews and where each puppy relieves itself.

If the puppies have no available toilet and the entire puppy area has been covered with sheets of newspaper, the puppies will have developed a strong preference for going on paper and will need specialized housetraining in their new home. Moreover, if there is

no toilet and the entire area has been littered with straw or shredded paper, the puppies will have learned they may eliminate anywhere and everywhere, which is what they will do in your home.
The longer the puppy has been raised in these conditions, the
more difficult it will be to housetrain.

- Check for the use of several hollow chewtoys (such as
  Kongs, Biscuit Balls, or sterilized bones) stuffed with
  kibble.

- Check for the use of a doggy toilet in the puppies' living area. Comparing how many piles and puddles are
  in the toilet versus on the floor will offer a good indication of where the puppy will eliminate when she
  comes to your home.

BASIC MANNERS

Inquire about the litter's ongoing obedience training program and
ask the breeder to demonstrate the puppies' basic obedience skills,
for example, to come, sit, lie down, and roll over.

- Evaluate each puppy's response to your lure/reward
  training attempts using pieces of kibble and a Kong as
  lures and rewards. (To learn more about lure/reward
  training, see chapter 5.)

PERSONAL PREFERENCE

When choosing the puppy, it is so important that all family members agree. You want to select the puppy you all like best, and you
want to select a puppy who likes all of you. Sit down quietly as a
family and see which puppies make contact first and which ones
stay around the longest.

For years it was dogmatically stated that puppies who approached quickly, jumped up, and bit your hands were totally unsuitable as pets, since they were aggressive and difficult to train. On the contrary, these are normal, well-socialized eight-week-old puppies who are simply saying hello in true puppy fashion without the benefit of manners. With some very basic training to redirect the pup's delightful exuberance, you'll have the fastest recalls and the quickest sits in puppy class. Also, puppy biting is both normal and absolutely necessary. In fact the more dogs bite as puppies, the softer and safer their jaws in adulthood. (For more information about bite inhibition, please see chapter 7.)

Spend at least two hours selecting a puppy. Eight-week-old pups cycle between extreme hyperactivity and total exhaustion every sixty minutes or so. Make sure you get a comprehensive impression of the puppy's total behavior repertoire.

I would be more concerned about puppies who were slow to approach or remained in hiding. It is completely, utterly, and absolutely *abnormal* for a well-socialized six- to eight-week-old puppy to be shy when approaching people. If the puppy acts shy or scared, then without a doubt she has not been sufficiently socialized. Look elsewhere. If, however, you really have your heart set on taking a shy puppy, only do so if each family member can coax the pup to approach and take a food treat. A shy puppy represents a substantial time commitment, since she will need to be handfed kibble every day from a variety of strangers. To rehabilitate this pup, you'll certainly have your work cut out for you during the next four weeks.

Beware of breeders who want to decide for you whether to raise your pup for conformation shows or have it neutered. Remember, the puppy is coming to live with you. Raising the pup is your responsibility, and decisions regarding its show career and reproductive status are yours to make.

You can enjoy numerous wonderful activities with your neutered dog, including competitive, rally, and freestyle obedience. Others include agility, carting, flyball, Frisbee, K9 Games, search and rescue, sledding, tracking, and of course, dog walks and trips to the dog park.

It's entirely your choice, but please consider neutering your puppy. Each year, millions of puppies and young adult dogs are euthanized (killed) in animal shelters. It's simply not fair for puppies, and it is not fair for animal-loving shelter personnel. Please don't add to the numbers. Please neuter your puppy.

SINGLETON PUPPIES

Most pups have adequate opportunity to play with their littermates during their first eight weeks. Singleton and hand-reared pups have had insufficient opportunity to play (play-fight and play-bite) and therefore teaching bite inhibition is a top priority.

Enroll in a puppy class as soon as your puppy reaches three months of age. Play and socialization are essential for puppies to develop and maintain a soft mouth.

COMMON PITFALLS

"Our last dog was perfectly trustworthy."

Maybe you were just lucky and picked a born-to-be-perfect puppy. Or maybe you were an excellent trainer. But can you still remember what you did back then and do you still have the time to do it?

"Our last dog just loved kids!"

One young family doted on their first dog and devoted a lot of time to its training. The whole family attended puppy classes and held puppy parties at home for the children's friends. So many children spent time playing games and reward-training the dog that of course the dog loved children. The dog enjoyed her sunset years proudly watching the children grow up and graduate from high school. By the time the parents got their second dog, the children had all left the nest. The new puppy grows up in a world without children. All is well for many years — that is, until grandchildren appear on the scene.

IF YOU REALLY WANT A HOUSETRAINING CHALLENGE

If you really want to set yourself a housetraining challenge, buy a three-month-old puppy from a pet store window littered with shredded paper and straw with no specific toilet area. This puppy has been trained to eliminate anywhere, anytime. And that's exactly what it will do when you get it home. You'll be cleaning up urine and feces for a very long time!

REMEMBER

You are choosing a pup to come and live in your home and adapt to your lifestyle, so please make sure the puppy has been prepared for domestic life in general and is suitable for your lifestyle in particular. Beware of statements like:

"We haven't taught the puppies to sit because they are showdogs."

Basically this breeder is under the impression the dog is so dumb it cannot tell the difference between two simple instructions such as "Sit" and "Stand." Look elsewhere. Just because the breeder is prepared to live with dogs who haven't even been taught to sit does not mean to say you should! Also, if the puppy hasn't even been taught basic manners, there are probably many other things the breeder has failed to teach.

"He's the scaredy-cat of the litter."

Certainly in any litter individual dogs will display different tendencies toward approaching strangers (you), but no eight-week-old puppy should be scared to approach people. Any shyness, fearfulness, or tendency to avoid people should have been noticed and dealt with as early as four weeks ago. The shy puppy should have been supersocialized. A single scaredy-cat puppy in a litter indicates that the breeder has not been vigilant in assessing day-to-day socialization. There are most probably other good puppies in the litter, but I suggest that you be vigilant when assessing their socialization status.

Errorless Housetraining and Chewtoy-Training

(The First Day Your Puppy Comes Home)

WHAT TO TEACH YOUR PUPPY DURING HIS FIRST WEEK AT HOME

Your canine newcomer is just itching to learn household manners. He wants to please, but he has to learn how. Before the young pup can be trusted to have full run of the house, somebody must teach the house rules. Otherwise, your puppy will let his imagination run wild in his quest for occupational therapy to pass the time of day. Without a firm grounding in canine domestic etiquette, your puppy will be left to improvise in his choice of toys and toilets. The pup will no doubt eliminate in closets and on carpets, and your couches and curtains will be viewed as playthings for destruction. If your pup is allowed to make "mistakes," bad habits will quickly become the status quo. Then it becomes necessary to break bad habits before teaching good habits.

Your puppy's living quarters need to be designed so that housetraining and chewtoy-training are errorless. Each mistake is a dire warning, since it predicts many more to come.

ERRORLESS HOUSETRAINING
AND CHEWTOY-TRAINING

Successful domestic doggy education involves teaching your puppy to train itself through confinement. This prevents mistakes and establishes good habits from the outset. When you are physically or mentally absent, confine your puppy to keep him out of mischief and to help him learn how to act appropriately.

The more you confine your puppy to his Doggy Den and Puppy Playroom during his first few weeks at home, the more freedom he will enjoy as an adult dog for the rest of his life. The more closely you follow the following puppy-confinement program, the sooner your puppy will be housetrained and chewtoy-trained. And, as an added benefit, your puppy will learn to settle down quickly, quietly, calmly, and happily.

WHEN YOU ARE NOT AT HOME

Keep your puppy confined to a fairly small puppy playroom, such as the kitchen, bathroom, or utility room. You can also use an exercise pen to cordon off a small section of a room. This is his long-term confinement area. It should include:

1. A comfortable bed

2. A bowl of fresh water

3. Plenty of hollow chewtoys (stuffed with dog food)

4. A doggy toilet in the farthest corner from his bed

Obviously, your puppy will feel the need to bark, chew, and eliminate throughout the course of the day, and so he must be left somewhere he can satisfy his needs without causing any damage or annoyance. Your puppy will most probably eliminate as far as possible from his sleeping quarters, in his doggy toilet. By removing all chewable items from the puppy playpen — with the exception of hollow chewtoys stuffed with kibble — you will make chewing chewtoys your puppy's favorite habit, a good habit! Long-term confinement allows your puppy to teach itself to use an appropriate dog toilet, to want to chew appropriate chewtoys, and to settle down quietly.

When you are not at home, confine your puppy to a playroom with a comfortable bed, a bowl of water, stuffed chewtoys, and a doggy toilet.

THE PURPOSE OF LONG-TERM CONFINEMENT

1. To confine the puppy to an area where chewing and toilet behavior are acceptable so the puppy does not make any chewing or housesoiling mistakes around the house.

2. To maximize the likelihood that the puppy will learn to use the provided toilet, to chew only chewtoys (the only chewables available in the playroom), and to settle down calmly without barking.

WHEN YOU ARE AT HOME

Enjoy short play and training sessions hourly. If you cannot pay full attention to your puppy's every single second, play with your pup in his Puppy Playpen, where a suitable toilet and toys are available. Or, for periods of no longer than an hour at a time, confine your puppy to his doggy den, or short-term close confinement area, such as a portable dog crate. Every hour, release your puppy and quickly take him to his doggy toilet. Your puppy's short-term confinement area should include a comfortable bed, and plenty of hollow chewtoys (stuffed with dog food).

It is much easier to watch your pup if he is settled down in a single spot. Either you may move the crate so that your puppy is in the same room as you, or you may want to confine your pup to a different room to start preparing him for times when he will be left at home alone. If you do not like the idea of confining your puppy to a dog crate, you may tie the leash to your belt and have the pup settle down at your feet. Or you may fasten the leash to an eye hook in the baseboard next to your puppy's bed, basket, or mat. To prevent the chewtoys from rolling out of reach, also tie them to the eye hook.

When you are at home, confine your puppy to a dog crate with some stuffed chewtoys. Every hour take your puppy to an appropriate toilet area and it will eliminate within seconds — two minutes max!

THE PURPOSE OF SHORT-TERM CLOSE CONFINEMENT

1. To prevent chewing or housesoiling mistakes around the house.

2. To make the puppy a chewtoyaholic (since chewtoys are the only chewables available and they are stuffed with food) and to teach the puppy to settle down calmly and happily for periodic quiet moments.

3. To predict when the puppy needs to eliminate. Dogs naturally avoid soiling their den, so closely confining a puppy to its bed temporarily inhibits urination and defecation. This means the pup will need to relieve itself when released from the crate each hour. You will then be there to show the puppy the right spot, reward her for eliminating in the right spot, and then enjoy a short play/training session with the delightfully empty puppy.

TRAIN YOUR PUPPY TO TRAIN ITSELF

Housetraining and chewtoy-training will be quick and easy if you adhere to the puppy confinement plan above, which prevents the puppy from making mistakes and prompts the puppy to teach itself household etiquette. If you vary from the program you will likely experience problems. Unless you enjoy problems, you must reprimand *yourself* for any mistakes you allow your puppy to make.

Most dog crates are portable and may easily be moved from room to room so that when you are at home, your puppy learns to settle down quickly and amuse herself quietly. Then you can settle down and amuse yourself and read a book in the living room . . .

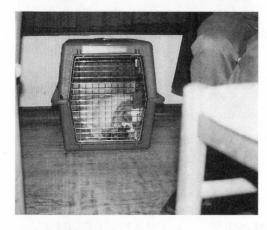

. . . eat dinner in the dining room . . .

. . . or work at the computer.

ERRORLESS HOUSETRAINING

Housesoiling is a spatial problem, involving perfectly normal, natural, and necessary canine behaviors (peeing and pooping) performed in inappropriate places.

Housetraining is quickly and easily accomplished by praising your puppy and offering a food treat when he eliminates in an appropriate toilet area. Once your pup realizes that his eliminatory products are the equivalent of coins in a food vending machine — that feces and urine may be cashed in for tasty treats — your pup will be clamoring to eliminate in the appropriate spot, because soiling the house does not bring equivalent fringe benefits.

Housesoiling is also a temporal problem: either the puppy is in the wrong place at the right time (confined indoors with full bladder and bowels), or the puppy is in the right place at the wrong time (outdoors in the yard or on a walk, but with empty bladder and bowels).

Timing is the essence of successful housetraining. Indeed, efficient and effective housetraining depends upon the owner being able to predict when the puppy needs to eliminate so that he may be directed to an appropriate toilet area and more than adequately rewarded for doing the right thing in the right place at the right time.

Usually, puppies urinate within half a minute of waking up from a nap and usually defecate within a couple of minutes of that. But who has the time to hang around to wait for puppy to wake up and pee and poop? Instead it's a better plan to wake up the puppy yourself, when you are ready and the time is right.

Short-term confinement offers a convenient means to accurately predict when your puppy needs to relieve itself. Confining a pup to a small area strongly inhibits him from urinating or defecating since he doesn't want to soil his sleeping area. Hence, the puppy is highly likely to want to eliminate immediately after being released from confinement.

HOUSETRAINING IS AS EASY AS 1-2-3

When you are away from home or if you are too busy or distracted to adhere to the following schedule, keep your puppy confined to its puppy playroom, where she has a suitable doggy toilet. Otherwise, when you are at home:

1. Keep your puppy closely confined to her doggy den (crate) or on-leash.

2. Every hour on the hour release your pup from confinement and quickly run her (on-leash if necessary) to the toilet area, instruct your pup to eliminate, and give her three minutes to do so.

3. Enthusiastically praise your puppy when she eliminates, offer three freeze-dried liver treats, and then play/train with the pup indoors; once your puppy is old enough to go outside, take her for a walk after she eliminates.

SOME COMMON PITFALLS

If errorless housetraining is so easy, why do so many dog owners experience problems? Here are some common questions and answers that help make errorless housetraining work:

Why confine the pup to his doggy den? Why not his playroom?

Short-term close confinement allows you to predict when your puppy wants to go so that you may be there to direct him to the appropriate spot and reward him for doing the right thing in the right place at the right time. During the hour-long periods of close confinement, as your puppy lies doggo in dreamy repose, his bladder and bowels are slowly but surely filling up. Whenever the big hand reaches twelve and you dutifully release the pup to run to his indoor toilet or backyard doggy toilet to relieve himself, your puppy is likely to eliminate pronto. Knowing when your puppy wants to go allows you to choose the spot and most importantly to reward your puppy handsomely for using it. Rewarding your puppy for using his toilet is the secret to successful house-training. If on the other hand the puppy were left in his playroom, he would most likely use his indoor toilet but would not be rewarded for doing so.

What if my puppy doesn't like going in her crate?

Before confining your puppy to her crate (doggy den), you first need to teach her to love the crate and confinement. This is so easy to do. Stuff a couple of hollow chewtoys with kibble and the occasional treat. Let your puppy sniff the stuffed chewtoys and then place them in the crate and shut the door with your puppy on the outside. Usually it takes just a few seconds for your puppy to beg you to open the door and let her inside. In no time at all, your pup will be happily preoccupied with her chewtoys.

When leaving the puppy in her long-term confinement area, tie the stuffed chewtoys to the inside of the crate and leave the crate door open. Thus, the puppy can choose whether she wants to explore the small area or lie down on her bed in her crate and try to extricate the kibble and treats from her chewtoys. Basically, the stuffed chewtoys are confined to the crate and the puppy is given the option of coming or going at will. Most puppies choose to rest comfortably inside the crate with stuffed chewtoys for entertainment. This technique works especially well if your puppy is not fed kibble from a bowl but only from chewtoys or by hand, as lures and rewards in training. To use this method, each morning measure out the puppy's daily ration of food into a bag to avoid overfeeding.

Before confining your puppy, make sure that he enjoys spending time in his crate. Feeding all of his dinner kibble stuffed into Kongs inside his crate usually does the trick within a couple of days. The following technique works even quicker. Have your puppy sit while you open the crate door...

...place a stuffed Kong inside the crate and close the door...

...with your puppy on the outside! Let the pup dwell on his dilemma — stuffed Kong inside and puppy locked outside — and then after a while, open the crate door...

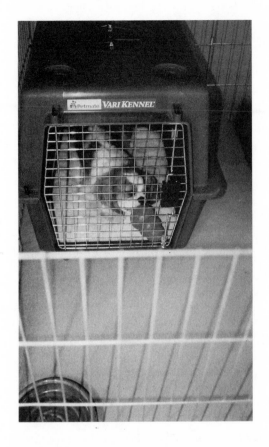

. . . and your puppy will eagerly dash inside the crate and quickly settle down to chew his chewtoy.

What if I don't like putting my puppy in a crate?

Short-term confinement, whether to a crate or tie-down, is a temporary training measure to help you teach your puppy where to eliminate and what to chew. A dog crate is the best housetraining tool to help you accurately predict when your dog wishes to relieve himself and is the best training tool to help you to teach your puppy to become a chewtoyaholic. Once your puppy has learned to eliminate only in appropriate areas and to chew only appropriate objects, he may be given free run of the house and garden for the rest of his life. You will probably find, however, that after just a few days your puppy learns to love his crate and will voluntarily rest inside. Your puppy's very own den is a quiet, comfortable, and special doggy place.

If, on the other hand, your puppy is given unsupervised free run of the house from the outset, the odds are that it will be confined later on — first to the yard, then to the basement, then to a cage in an animal shelter, and then to a coffin. Without a doubt, housesoiling and destructive chewing are the two most prevalent terminal illnesses in dogs. Using a dog crate will help you prevent these problems from ever developing in your puppy.

Why not just leave the puppy outdoors until it is housetrained?

Who is going to housetrain your pup outside — a shrub? If the puppy is left outside unattended, she will become an indiscriminate eliminator. Basically, your puppy will learn to go wherever she wants, whenever she wants, and she will likely do the same whenever you let her indoors. Puppies left outdoors and unsupervised for long periods of time seldom become housetrained. Also, they tend to become indiscriminate barkers, chewers, diggers, and escapists, and they may be more easily stolen. Outdoor puppies also become so excited on the few occasions they are invited indoors that eventually they are no longer allowed inside at all.

Why release the pup every hour? Why not every 55 minutes, or every three hours? Is it really necessary to do it on the hour?

Puppies have a 45-minute bladder capacity at three weeks of age, 75-minute capacity at eight weeks, 90-minute capacity at twelve weeks, and, two-hour capacity at eighteen weeks. Releasing your puppy every hour offers you an hourly opportunity to reward your dog for using a designated toilet area. You do not have to do this precisely each hour, but it is much easier to remember to do so each hour on the hour.

Why run the puppy to the toilet? Why not walk sedately?

If you take your time getting your puppy to his doggy toilet, you may find that he pees or poops en route. Hurrying your puppy tends to jiggle his bowels and bladder so that he really wants to go the moment you let him stand still and sniff his toilet area.

Why not just put the puppy outside? Can't she do it on her own?

Of course she can. But the whole point of predicting when your puppy wants to relieve herself is so you can show her where and offer well-deserved praise and reward. Thus your puppy will learn where you would like her to go. Also, if you see your puppy eliminate, you know that she is empty; you may then allow your empty puppy supervised exploration of the house for a while before returning her to her den.

Why instruct the pup to eliminate? Doesn't he know he wants to go?

By instructing your puppy to eliminate beforehand and by rewarding him for eliminating afterward, you will teach your pup to go on command. Eliminating on cue is a boon when you are traveling with your dog and in other time-constrained situations. Ask your pup to "Hurry up," "Do your business," or "Go pee and poop," or use some other socially acceptable, euphemistic eliminatory command.

Why give the puppy three minutes? Isn't one minute sufficient?

Usually, a young pup will urinate within thirty seconds of being released from short-term confinement, but it may take one or two minutes for her to defecate. It is certainly worthwhile to allow your pup three minutes to complete her business.

What if the puppy doesn't go?

Your puppy will be more likely to eliminate if you stand still and let him circle around you on-leash. If your puppy does not eliminate within the allotted time, no biggie! Simply pop the pup back in his crate and try again in half an hour. Repeat the process over and over until he does eliminate. Eventually, your puppy will eliminate outdoors and you will be able to reward him. Therefore,

on subsequent hourly trips to its toilet your puppy will be likely to
eliminate promptly.

Why praise the puppy? Isn't relief sufficient reward?

It is far better to express your emotions when praising your
puppy for getting it right than when reprimanding the poor pup
for getting it wrong. So really praise that pup: "Goooooooooood
puppy!" Housetraining is no time for understated thank-yous.
Don't be embarrassed about praising your puppy. Embarrassed dog
owners usually end up with housesoiling problems. Really reward
your puppy. Tell your puppy that he has done a most wonderful
and glorious thing!

Why offer treats? Isn't praise sufficient reward?

In a word, no! Many owners — especially men — seem inca-
pable of convincingly praising their puppies. Consequently,
it might be a good idea to give the pup a food treat or two (or
three) for his effort. Input for output! "Wow! My owner's great.
Every time I pee or poop outside, she gives me a treat. I never
get yummy treats when I do it on the couch. I can't wait for my
owner to come home so I can go out in the yard and cash in
my urine and feces for food treats!" In fact, why not keep some
treats in a screw-top jar handy to the doggy toilet?

Why freeze-dried liver?

Housetraining is one of those times when you want to pull
out all of the stops. Take my word for it: when it comes to housetraining, use the Ferrari of dog treats — freeze-dried liver.

*Do we really have to give three liver treats when the puppy pees or poops?
Isn't this a wee bit anal retentive?*

Yes and no. Certainly you do not have to give your puppy
exactly three treats every time. But it's a funny thing: If I suggest

that people offer a treat each time their puppy eliminates promptly in the right place, they rarely follow instructions. Whenever I tell people to give three treats, however, they will painstakingly count out the treats to give to their puppy. Here's what I am trying to say: Handsomely praise and reward your puppy every time she uses a designated toilet area.

Why play with the puppy indoors?

If you reward your pup for using her doggy toilet, you will know she is empty. "Thank you, empty puppy!" What better time to play with or train your puppy indoors without facing the risk of a messy mistake. Why get a puppy unless you want to spend some quality (feces-free) time with her?

Why bother to take an older puppy outdoors for a walk when she's empty?

Many people fall into the trap of taking their puppy outside or walking it so that she may eliminate, and when she does they bring her indoors. Usually it takes just a couple of trials before the puppy learns, "Whenever my urine or feces hits the ground, my walk ends!" Consequently, the pup becomes reluctant to eliminate outside, and so when brought home after a long jiggling play or walk, she is in dire need to relieve herself. Which she does. It is a much better plan to praise your puppy for using her doggy toilet and then take her for a walk as an additional reward for eliminating.

Get in the habit of taking an older puppy to her doggy toilet (in your yard or curbside in front of your apartment building), standing still, and waiting for the pup to eliminate. Praise the pup and offer liver treats when she does: "Good girl, let's go walkies!" Clean up and dispose of the feces in your own trash can, and then go and enjoy a poopless walk with your dog. After just a few days with a simple "no poop means no walk" rule, you'll find you have the quickest urinator and defecator in town.

What should I do if I've done all the above and I catch the puppy in the act of making a mistake?

Pick up a rolled newspaper and give yourself a smack! Obviously you did not follow the instructions above. Who allowed the urine-and-feces-filled puppy to have free-range access to your house? You! Should you ever reprimand or punish your puppy when you catch him in the act, all he will learn is to eliminate in secret — that is, never again in your untrustworthy presence. Thus you will have created an owner-absent housesoiling problem. If you ever catch your pup in the act of making a mistake that was your fault, at the very most you can quickly, softly, but urgently implore your pup, "Outside, outside, outside!" The tone and urgency of your voice communicate that you want your puppy to do something promptly, and the meaning of the words instructs the puppy where. Your response will have limited effect on the present mistake, but it helps prevent future mistakes.

Never reprimand your dog in a manner that is not instructive. Nonspecific reprimands only create more problems (owner-absent misbehavior) as well as frightening the pup and eroding the puppy-owner relationship. Your puppy is not a "bad puppy." On the contrary, your puppy is a good puppy that has been forced to misbehave because its owner could not, or would not, follow simple instructions.

Please reread and follow the above instructions!

Every hour on the hour, take your puppy to her toilet area — either her permanent toilet in the yard or the temporary toilet in her long-term confinement area — and handsomely reward the pup as soon as she eliminates.

THE DOGGY TOILET

For the best doggy toilet, equip a litter box or a piece of old linoleum with what will be the dog's eventual toilet material. For example, for rural and suburban pups who will eventually be taught to relieve themselves outside on earth or grass, lay down a roll of turf. Or, if you use puppy pads, rub a little soil or grass into the top of the pad. For urban puppies who will eventually be taught to eliminate at curbside, lay down a couple of thin concrete tiles. Your puppy will soon develop very strong substrate or olfactory preferences for eliminating on similarly smelling outdoor surfaces whenever she can.

If you have a backyard, in addition to the indoor playroom toilet, take your pup to his outdoor toilet in the yard whenever you release him from his doggy den. If you live in an apartment and do not have a yard, teach your puppy to use his indoor toilet until he is old enough to venture outdoors at three months of age.

TRAINING YOUR DOG TO USE AN OUTDOOR TOILET

For the first few weeks, take your puppy outside on-leash. Hurry to her toilet area and then stand still to allow the puppy to circle (as it would normally do before eliminating). Reward your puppy each time she "goes" in the designated spot. If you have a fenced yard, you may later take your puppy outside off-leash and let her choose where she would like to eliminate. But make sure to reward her differentially according to how close she hits ground zero. Offer one treat for doing it outside quickly, two treats for doing it within, say, five yards of the doggy toilet, three treats for within two yards, and five treats for a bull's-eye.

PROBLEMS

If you're using the methods above, yet still having problems with housesoiling or house destruction after one week, please consult my *Housetraining* and *Chewing* behavior booklets, available from James & Kenneth Publishers (1-800-784-5531 or www.jamesandkenneth.com).

ERRORLESS CHEWTOY-TRAINING

The dog is a social and inquisitive animal. He needs to do something, especially if left at home alone. What would you like your dog to do? Crosswords? Needlepoint? Watch soaps on the telly? You must provide some form of occupational therapy for your puppy to pass the day. If your puppy learns to enjoy chewing chewtoys, he will look forward to settling down quietly for some quality chewing time. It is important to teach your puppy to enjoy chewing chewtoys more than chewing household items. An effective ploy is to stuff the puppy's chewtoys with kibble and treats. In fact, during your puppy's first few weeks at home, put away his food bowl and, apart from using kibble as lures and rewards for training, serve all your puppy's kibble stuffed in hollow chewtoys — Kongs, Biscuit Balls, and sterilized bones.

For errorless chewtoy-training, adhere to the puppy confinement program. When away from home, leave the puppy in his puppy playroom with bed, water, toilet, and plenty of stuffed chewtoys. While at home, leave the puppy in his doggy den with plenty of stuffed chewtoys. Every hour after releasing the pup to relieve himself, play chewtoy games — chewtoy search, chewtoy fetch, and chewtoy tug-o'-war. Your puppy will soon develop a very strong chewtoy habit because you have limited his chewing choices to a single acceptable toy, which you have made even more attractive with the addition of kibble and treats.

Once your dog has become a chewtoyaholic and has not had a chewing (or housesoiling) mishap for at least one month, you may increase your puppy's playroom to two rooms. For each subsequent month without a mistake your puppy may gain access to another room, until eventually she enjoys free run of the entire house and garden when left at home alone. If a chewing mistake should occur, go back to the original puppy confinement program for at least a month.

In addition to preventing household destruction, teaching your puppy to become a chewtoyaholic prevents her from becoming a recreational barker, because chewing and barking are obviously mutually exclusive behaviors. Also, chewtoyaholism helps your puppy learn to settle down calmly because chewing and dashing about are mutually exclusive behaviors.

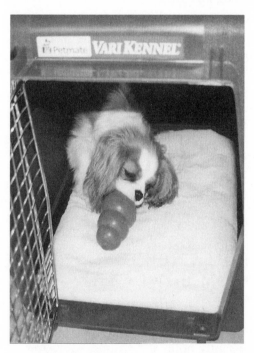

During his first couple of weeks at home, unless you are training or playing with your puppy, make sure he spends all of his time in his long-term or short-term confinement area, where the only available chewable objects are chewtoys stuffed with kibble and the occasional treat.

Chewtoyaholism is especially useful for dogs with Obsessive-Compulsive Disorder, since it provides them with an acceptable and convenient means to work out their obsessions and compulsions. Your dog may still have OCD, but a chewtoyaholic will happily spend its time obsessively and compulsively chewing her stuffed chewtoys!

Most important, chewtoy chewing keeps the puppy occupied and effectively helps prevent the development of separation anxiety.

WHAT IS A CHEWTOY?

A chewtoy is an object for the dog to chew that is neither destructible nor consumable. If your dog destroys an object, you will have to replace it, and that costs money. If your dog consumes the object, you may have to replace your dog. Eating nonfood items is extremely hazardous to your dog's health.

The type of chewtoy you choose will depend on your dog's penchant for chewing and its individual preferences. I have seen some dogs make a cow's hoof or a compressed rawhide chewy last forever, whereas other dogs consume them in a matter of minutes. I've found Kong products to be the Cadillacs of chewtoys. Hollow sterilized long bones are a very close second choice. I like Kong products and sterilized bones because they are simple, natural, and organic — not plastic. Also, being hollow, they can be stuffed with food. Kong products and sterilized bones are obtainable from any good pet supply store.

DINNER FROM CHEWTOYS, NOT FROM BOWLS

Customarily, puppies receive their entire daily allotment of kibble at dinner, which often becomes an unintentional jackpot reward for boisterously barking and expectantly bouncing around. Moreover, if you allow your puppy to wolf down dinner from a bowl, she will be at a loss for what to do for the rest of the day. In the wild, dogs spend a good 90 percent of their waking hours searching for food, so in a sense, regular bowl-feeding deprives a dog of her principal activity — searching for food. Instead, your inquisitive puppy will search for entertainment all day long. Most likely you will consider your puppy's choices of occupation to be mischievous misbehavior.

Squeaky toys are very effective lures and rewards in training, but . . . a squeaky toy is not a suitable chewtoy! Squeaky toys are both destructible and consumable. Allowing a young pup unsupervised play with intriguing and easily destroyed items will turn him into a destructive chewer in no time at all.

Chewtoys should be virtually indestructible, made of natural products (such as rubber or bone), and hollow (stuffable). Stuffing chewtoys with kibble and the occasional treat encourages the pup to focus on extricating the food, rather than on destroying the toy. Stuffing chewtoys prolongs their life expectancy. The very best chewtoys are Kongs, Biscuit Balls, and sterilized bones.

Once your dog has learned that designated chewtoys are the only appropriate chewtoys, he may be trusted to retrieve or play with other items. Ivan had a footwear fetish. He loved retrieving slippers and shoes, carrying slippers and shoes, and snuggling and sleeping with slippers and shoes. But he never destroyed them, and he could always find them when they were misplaced.

Without a doubt, regularly feeding a new puppy (or adult dog) from a bowl is a huge mistake in dog husbandry and training. Although unintentional, the effects of bowl-feeding are often severely detrimental for the puppy's household manners and sense of well-being. In a sense, each bowl-fed meal steals the puppy's raison d'être, its very reason for being. Within seconds of gulping his meal, the poor pup now faces a mental void for the rest of its day with nothing but long hours to worry and fret, or work himself into a frenzy.

As the puppy adapts to fill the void, normal behaviors such as chewing, barking, strolling, grooming, and playing become stereotypical, repetitive, and maladaptive. Specific behaviors increase in frequency until they no longer serve any useful function except to pass the time. Investigative chewing becomes destructive chewing. Alarm barking becomes incessant barking. Strolling from one place to another becomes repetitively pacing and circling. Investigating a shadow or light becomes a neurotic fixation. Routine grooming becomes excessive licking, scratching, tail-chasing, head-pressing, or in extreme cases, self-mutilation.

Stereotyped behaviors cause the release of endorphins, perpetuating their repetition, and in a sense, the dog becomes drugged and hooked on mindless, repetitive activity. Stereotyped behaviors are like behavioral cancers; they progressively increase in frequency and squeeze most useful and adaptive responses from the dog's behavior repertoire until eventually the "brain-dead" dog spends hours on end barking, pacing, chewing himself, or simply staring into space.

A vital facet of your puppy's early education is to teach him how to peacefully pass the time of day. Feeding your puppy's kibble only from hollow chewtoys — Kongs, Biscuit Balls, and sterilized bones — keeps your puppy happily occupied and content for hours on end. It allows the puppy to focus on an enjoyable activity so that he doesn't dwell on his loneliness. Each piece of extracted kibble also rewards your puppy for settling down calmly, for chewing an appropriate chewtoy, and for not barking.

CHEWTOY STUFFING

An old chewtoy becomes immediately novel and exciting when stuffed with food. If you use kibble from your puppy's normal daily ration, your puppy will not put on weight. To protect your puppy's waistline, heart, and liver, it is important to minimize the use of treats in training. Use kibble as lures and rewards for teaching basic manners and reserve freeze-dried liver treats for initial housetraining, for meeting children, men, and strangers, as a garnish for stuffing Kongs (see below), and as an occasional jackpot reward for especially good behavior.

KONG STUFFING 101

The basic principle of Kong stuffing ensures that some food comes out quickly and easily to instantly reward your puppy for initially contacting her chewtoy; bits of food come out over a long period of time to periodically reward your puppy for continuing to chew; and some of the best bits never come out, so your puppy never loses interest. Squish a small piece of freeze-dried liver in the small hole in the tip of the Kong so your puppy will never be able to get it out. Smear a little honey around the inside of the Kong, fill it up with kibble, and then block the big hole with crossed dog biscuits.

There are numerous creative variations on basic Kong stuffing. One of my favorite recipes comprises moistening your puppy's kibble, spooning it into the Kong, and then putting it in the freezer overnight — a Kongsicle! Your dog will love it.

KONG IS KING!

If from the outset you always confine your puppy with a selection of stuffed Kongs and Biscuit Balls, chewing these appropriate chewtoys will soon become an integral part of its day. Your puppy will

quickly develop a socially acceptable Kong habit. And remember, good habits are just as hard to break as bad habits. Your puppy will now spend a large part of its day musing over his Kong products.

Let's pause for a moment to consider all the bad things your puppy will not be doing if he is quietly engaged with his chewtoys. He will not be chewing inappropriate household and garden items. He will not be a recreational barker. (He will still bark when strangers come to the house, but he will not spend all day barking for barking's sake.) And he will not be running around, fretting, and working himself up when left at home alone.

The wonderful thing about teaching a puppy to enjoy chewing chewtoys is that this activity excludes many alternative, extremely annoying puppy behaviors. A stuffed Kong is one of the best stress-relievers, especially for anxious, obsessive, and compulsive dogs. (A Kong for a dog is also one of the best stress-relievers for the owner.) There is no single device that so easily and so simply prevents or resolves so many bad habits and behavior problems.

SETTLE DOWN AND SHUSH

High on the educational agenda is to teach your pup that there are times for play and times for quiet. Specifically, you want to teach the youngster to settle down and shush for short periods. Your life will be more peaceful, and your pup's life will be less stressful once she learns that frequent little quiet moments are the name of the game in her new home.

Beware of the trap of smothering your new puppy with non-stop attention and affection during her first days at home, for then she will whine, bark, and fret when left alone at night or during the daytime when you are at work and the children are at school. Of course the pup is lonely! This is her first time alone without her mother, littermates, or human companionship.

You can really help to ease your pup's anxiety by getting her used to settling down alone during her first few days at home. Remember, first impressions are very important and long lasting. Also keep in mind that the average suburban puppy will likely spend many hours and days left to her own devices. So it is well worthwhile to teach the pup how to spend time by herself. Otherwise, the puppy may become anxious when left alone and develop hard-to-break chewing, barking, digging, and escaping habits.

Chihuahua puppies are hardly Olympic destructive chewers, but they sure can yip. A stuffed Kong will teach her to settle down quickly, calmly. . . and quietly.

When you are at home confine your puppy to her doggy den with lots of chewtoys for housetraining, chewtoy-training, and teaching the pup to settle down peacefully and happily. It is important to confine your puppy for short periods when you are home in order to teach her how to enjoy her own company when left at home alone.

I am certainly not advocating leaving puppies alone for long periods of time. But it is a fact of modern day life that many puppy owners leave home each day to work for a living, so it is only fair to prepare the pup for this.

To get your puppy used to settling down off-leash, tie a stuffed Kong to an eye hook in the baseboard close to her bed next to the TV. It is easy to watch television and keep an eye on the pup at the same time. Do remember, though, the puppy still needs to be taken to her toilet area every hour.

When you are at home, the key is short-term confinement. The idea is not to lock up the puppy for hours on end, but rather to teach her to settle down quickly in a variety of settings and be confined for variable but mostly fairly short periods. Make sure the only objects within reach are stuffed chewtoys. And let me repeat: a puppy happily preoccupied with a stuffed chewtoy is not destroying household articles and furniture and is not barking.

When you are at home it is also a good idea to occasionally confine your puppy to her puppy playroom (long-term confinement area) as a practice run for your absence. Occasional long-term confinement when you are at home allows you to monitor your pup's behavior so you have some idea how she will act when you are gone.

HOME ALONE

A dog is not like a television or a video game. You can't just pull the plug or temporarily remove the batteries from a rambunctious puppy. Instead, you must teach him to settle down and shush. Right from the outset, make frequent quiet moments part of the puppy's daily routine. Following the confinement schedule described above will help your puppy train himself to settle down. Additionally, encourage your puppy to settle down beside you for longer and longer periods. For example, when you're watching television have your pup lie down on-leash or in his crate, but release him for short play-training breaks during the commercials.

When playing with your pup, have him settle down for frequent short interludes every fifteen seconds. Initially have the pup lie still for a few seconds before letting him play again. After fifteen seconds, interrupt the play session once more with a three-second settle-down. Then try for four seconds, then five, eight, ten, and so on. Although it's difficult at first, being yo-yoed between Settle Down and Let's Play, the puppy soon learns to settle down quickly and happily. Your puppy will learn that being asked to settle down is not the end of the world, nor is it necessarily the end of the play session, but instead that Settle Down signals a short time-out and reward break before he is allowed to resume playing.

If you teach your puppy to be calm and controlled when told, you will have years of fun and excitement ahead. Once your puppy has learned to settle down and shush on cue, there is so much more your dog can enjoy with you. Your well-trained dog is likely to be invited for many walks, trips in the car, picnics, visits to the pub, or to Grandma's, and even on incredible journeys to stay in ritzy dog-friendly hotels. On the other hand, if you let your dog play indiscriminately as a puppy, he will no doubt want to play indiscriminately as an adult. Your dog will be hyperactive and uncontrollable because you have unintentionally taught him to act that way. If your pup has not been taught to settle down by the time he reaches adolescence, he will be unfit to be taken places. Your pup will begin a lifetime of confinement and isolation at home while the rest of the family go out to have a good time. Not fair!

Since Claude was an anxious soul and a big-time destructive chewer, for the first ten days after adoption he was fed kibble only from chewtoys placed in his chewtoy basket.

Until you have trained your puppy to enjoy spending much of his day at home alone, you might recruit a puppy sitter. Just a few houses down the street, there may live an elderly person, for example, who would just love to live with a dog. He or she might be willing to come over during the daytime and sit and enjoy your TV or the contents of your fridge, maintain your puppy's confinement schedule, regularly reward him for using his doggy toilet, periodically play with the pup, and teach him household rules.

SEPARATION ANXIETY

Maintaining your puppy's confinement schedule when you are at home prepares your puppy to be calm when you are gone. Allowing a young puppy unrestricted access to you when you are at home quickly encourages her to become overly dependent, and overdependence is the most common reason why dogs become anxious when left at home alone.

Try your best to teach your puppy to enjoy her own company, to develop self-confidence, and to stand on her own four paws. Once your puppy is confident and relaxed when left alone, she may be allowed to spend all the time she wants with you when you are around.

When leaving your puppy for hourly sessions in her short-term confinement area or dog crate, make a point to check how she fares when left in another room. For example, periodically confine your puppy to her crate in the dining room while you prepare food in the kitchen, then keep the pup in her crate in the kitchen while the family eats dinner in the dining room.

Claude Konged — peacefully passing the time when left at home alone (after chewing himself to sleep).

WHEN LEAVING HOME

Make sure to stuff a number of chewtoys with kibble and treats. Make sure to stuff a piece of freeze-dried liver into the tiny hole of each Kong, or deep into the marrow cavity of each bone. Place the tastily stuffed chewtoys in your puppy's long-term confinement area and shut the door . . . with your puppy on the outside! When your puppy begs you to open the door, let him in and shut the door and leave quietly. Your puppy's chewing will be regularly reinforced by each piece of kibble that falls out of the chewtoy. Your puppy will continue to chew in an attempt to extract the freeze-dried liver. Eventually your puppy will fall asleep.

Additionally, leave a radio playing. The sound will provide white noise to mask outside disturbances. The sound of a radio is also reassuring, since it is normally associated with your presence. My malamute Phoenix was quite partial to classical music, country, and calypso. Oso preferred television, especially ESPN or CNN — the sound of reassuring male voices, perhaps? And Claude prefers Premiership soccer on Fox Sports World.

WHEN RETURNING HOME

Do not acknowledge your puppy's presence with praise or petting until she retrieves a chewtoy. Once she brings you a chewtoy, use a pen or pencil to push out the piece of freeze-dried liver your puppy has been unable to extract. This will impress your puppy to no end.

Dogs are crepuscular and quite happy to sleep all day and all night. As I've said, they have two activity peaks, at dawn and dusk. Thus, most chewing and barking activity is likely to occur right after you leave your pup in the morning and just before you return in the evening. Leaving your puppy with freshly stuffed chewtoys and offering the unextracted treats when you return prompts your puppy to seek out her chewtoys at times of peak activity.

JEKYLL-AND-HYDE BEHAVIOR

Smothering your puppy with attention and affection when you are home primes the pup to really miss you when you are gone. A Jekyll-and-Hyde environment (lots of attention when you are there, and none when you are gone) quickly creates a Jekyll-and-Hyde puppy that is completely confident when you are there but falls apart and panics when you are gone.

If you allow your puppy to become dependent upon your presence, he will be anxious in your absence. Canine anxiety is bad news for you and bad news for your pup. When stressed, dogs are more likely to indulge in bad habits, such as housesoiling, chewing, digging, and barking. Being anxious is also decidedly unpleasant for your dog.

Many supposed signs of separation anxiety are really signs of an insufficiently trained dog being allowed unsupervised free range of the house and encountering temptation left by his owners.

During your puppy's first few weeks at home, frequent confinement with stuffed chewtoys is essential for your pup to develop confidence and independence. Once your puppy is quite happy busying himself with his chewtoys whenever left alone, you may safely allow your now well-behaved and confident pup to enjoy as much time with you as he likes, without the fear that he will become anxious in your absence.

WONDERFUL WEEKENDS... AND WORRISOME WEEKDAYS

Whereas weekend attention and affection is wonderful, it primes your new puppy to miss the family on Monday morning when the parents go to work and the children leave for school. By all means, play with and train your puppy lots during the weekend, but also have lots of quiet moments to prepare your puppy for lonely weekdays.

IS IT REALLY SEPARATION ANXIETY?

Most doggy "disobedience" and wanton house destruction in the owner's absence has nothing to do with separation anxiety. In fact, separation *relief* might be a more precise and descriptive term. The dog chews, digs, barks, and soils the house only when the owner is absent because she has learned it would be foolhardy to indulge in

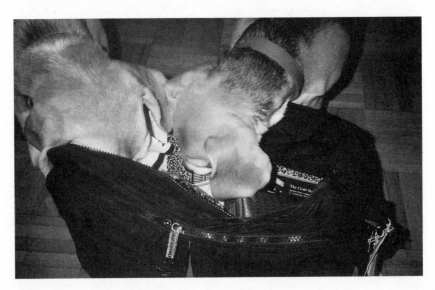

Beagles just begging to "unpack" a visitor's unattended luggage.

these pastimes when the owner is present. Owner-absent misbehavior is an indication that the owner has tried to suppress normal and natural dog behaviors with punishment, rather than teaching the dog how to behave — namely, how to express her basic doggy desires in an acceptable fashion. Often the term *separation anxiety* is an excuse for a dog who is simply not yet housetrained or chewtoy-trained.

WHAT TO DO AT NIGHTTIME

You choose where your pup sleeps at night. If you want your pup in his long-term confinement area overnight, or in a dog crate in the kitchen or your bedroom, that's fine. Or if you want the pup tethered in his bed beside your bed, that's fine too. What is important, though, is that the puppy is confined to a small area and settles down quickly and quietly. Offer the puppy an intelligently stuffed chewtoy and he will likely chew himself to sleep in no time at all.

Practice having your puppy settle down by your bed (or wherever you would like her to sleep at night) in the daytime. In other words, get your puppy used to sleeping peacefully alone before you plan to sleep peacefully.

Once you have housetrained and chewtoy-trained your puppy and he has learned to settle down quickly, you may allow your pup to choose where he would like to sleep — indoors, outdoors, upstairs, downstairs, in your bedroom, or in your bed — just as long as his choice is fine with you.

It is a good idea to practice the nighttime routine during the daytime when you are awake and in a good humor. Don't wait to train your puppy until you are tired and ready for bed and your grouchy brain is barely functioning. During the daytime, practice having your puppy settle down in his bed or crate both in the same room as you and in different rooms so that he gets used to sleeping alone.

Should your pup whine at nighttime, check on him every ten minutes. Talk softly to him and stroke him gently for a minute and then go back to bed. But do not overdo it. The idea is to reassure your puppy, not to train him to whine for late-night attention. Also, do not go straight to sleep, for you'll probably be checking on your puppy after ten minutes. Once the puppy eventually falls asleep, I find it enjoyable to check in on him and stroke him for four or five minutes. A lot of people dare not do this for fear they will wake the little critter, but it has always worked well for me. (It worked well with my son too.)

If you follow the above routine, you'll find it will take fewer than seven nights before your puppy learns to go to sleep quickly and quietly.

SIT, ETC.

I guess there would be more than a few disappointed owners if I didn't at least say something about training your dog to sit. Well, it's just so easy. Ask your puppy, "Would you like to learn to sit on request?" and then move a piece of kibble up and down in front of her nose. If your puppy nods in agreement, then you're both ready to proceed.

Say, "Puppy, Sit," and then move the kibble upwards and backwards along the top of her muzzle. As the puppy looks up to follow the kibble, she will sit down. Pretty simple, yes?

Now say, "Puppy, Down," and with another piece of kibble between finger and thumb, lower your hand, palm downward, to just in front of the dog's two forepaws. Your pup will lower her nose to investigate the kibble and then lower her forequarters with the side of her muzzle on the floor to nuzzle under your hand. Move the kibble slightly towards your puppy's chest, and her rear end will plop down.

Say, "Puppy, Sit," waggle a food lure in front of her nose and then raise the lure (palm upward) just a little. As the puppy looks up to follow the lure she will sit down. Praise the pup, "Good Sit," and offer the food as a reward.

Say, "Puppy, Down," and then lower the lure (palm downward) to just in front of the pup's forepaws. The puppy will lower her nose to follow the lure and then lie down. Praise the pup, "Good Down," and maybe offer the food as a reward.

Now say, "Puppy, Stand," and move the kibble forward away from your puppy. (You may have to waggle the kibble a little to reactivate the pup.) Hold the treat at nose level, but lower it a tad as soon as your pup stands up and starts to sniff; otherwise your pup will sit as soon as she stands.

Now try chaining a few commands together. Back up a couple of steps, say, "Puppy, Come Here," and wave the kibble. Enthusiastically praise your puppy as she approaches, and then ask her to sit and lie down before offering the kibble. Three responses for one piece of kibble — not bad, eh? Now have your puppy come, sit, and lie down as many times as there are spare moments in the day or as many pieces of kibble in the dog's dinner.

Say, "Puppy, Stand," and then move the food lure away from the pup's nose and waggle it. Praise the pup as soon as she stands up. Say, "Good Stand," and maybe offer the food as a reward.

Repetitively practice the above three positions in random sequences — Sit, Down, Sit, Stand, Down, Stand, etc. See how many position changes your pup is willing to do for just one food reward and how long you can keep the puppy in each position (short stays) before giving each food reward. Strangely enough, the fewer treats you give and the longer you keep each treat in your hand, the better your pup will learn. Welcome to the wonderful world of lure/reward training.

MISBEHAVIOR

Misbehavior is sadly a most prevalent terminal illness for pet dogs. Many puppies all but sign their death warrants during their very first week at home. Minor housesoiling and chewing mistakes lead to banishment to the back yard, where the dog develops severe socialization problems and learns to bark, dig, and escape. By the time the dog is picked up on the streets as an escapee or a latch-key stray or is surrendered to an animal shelter, he has developed so many behavior problems that he is not easily adoptable.

Sadly, all of these utterly predictable problems could be so easily prevented by owner and puppy education.

CHAPTER SIX

THE FOURTH DEVELOPMENTAL DEADLINE

Socialization with People

(By Three Months of Age)

Raising and training a pup to be people-friendly is the second most important goal of pet dog husbandry. (Remember, teaching bite inhibition is always the most important goal.) But during your pup's first month at home, urgency dictates that socialization with people is the prime puppy directive.

Your puppy must be fully socialized to people before he is three months old. Many people think puppy classes are the time to socialize puppies to people. Not so. It's too little, and too late. Puppy classes are a fun night out to continue socializing socialized puppies with people, for therapeutic socialization of puppies with other puppies, and most important, for puppies to learn bite inhibition.

You now have just a few weeks left to socialize your puppy. Unfortunately, your pup needs to be confined indoors until he is at least three months old, when he has acquired sufficient immunity through his puppy shots against the more serious dog diseases. However, even a relatively short period of social isolation at such a crucial developmental stage could damage your puppy's temperament. Whereas dog-dog socialization may be put on temporary hold until your pup is old enough to go to puppy school and the dog park, you simply cannot delay socialization with people. It may be possible to live with a dog who does not like other dogs, but it is difficult and potentially dangerous to live with a dog who does not like people, especially if the dog doesn't like some of your friends and family.

Consequently, there is considerable urgency to introducing your puppy to a wide variety of people — to family, friends, strangers, and especially men and children. As a rule of thumb, your pup needs to meet at least a hundred different people before he is three months old — an average of three unfamiliar people a day.

URGENCY

From the very first day you get your puppy, the clock is ticking. And time flies! By eight weeks of age, your puppy's Critical Period of Socialization is already waning and within a month, his most impressionable learning period will start to close. There is so much to teach and nearly everything needs to be taught right away.

BE SAFE

Puppies may become infected with serious dog diseases by sniffing the urine or feces of infected dogs. Never let your puppy on the ground where other dogs may have eliminated. You may take your puppy for car rides and to visit friends, but always carry your puppy from house to car, and vice versa. Of course, these precautions also apply to visits to the veterinary clinic. The ground immediately outside the door of the clinic and the floor of the waiting room are two of the most likely contaminated areas. Carry your puppy from the car to the clinic and keep him on your lap in the waiting room. Better yet, keep your puppy crated in your car until it is time for his examination.

DOGGY DREAM OR NASTY NIGHTMARE?

The most important quality in a pet dog is his temperament. A dog with a good temperament can be a dream to live with, but a dog with a tricky temperament is a perpetual nightmare. Moreover, regardless of breed or breeding, a dog's temperament, especially his feelings toward people and other dogs, is primarily the result of his level of socialization during puppyhood, the most important time in a dog's life. Do not waste this golden opportunity. Solid gold temperaments are forged during this period.

A HUNDRED PEOPLE

Capitalize on the time your pup needs to be confined indoors by inviting people to your home. I know that having your pup meet a hundred different people before he is three months old sounds almost impossible. But it is actually quite easy to accomplish. Twice a week, invite different groups of six men to watch sports on TV.

Not a bad start. Eighteen people to meet one two-month-old puppy at home.

Lure the men with the prospect of television sports programs, pizza, and beer. On several other nights a week, invite different groups of six women for ice cream, chocolate, and good conversation. (Or the other way around — you know your friends better than I do.) On another night of the week, catch up on all of your outstanding social obligations by inviting family, friends, and neighbors for meet-the-puppy dinners. If your work allows it, another tactic is to bring your puppy to visit your office for the day. Or, have a puppy party once a week. Above all, don't keep your puppy a secret. One of the great things about puppy socialization is that it also does wonders for your social life!

SAMPLE INVITATION:

Mr. Nice Guy

is cordially invited to a

Meet-the-Puppy Party

7:30–9:00 pm • March 7th

Please come and help my puppy

learn to love men.

Healthy gourmet food, premium beverages,

and televised sports will be provided.

Please bring an additional adult male human.

R.S.V.P. (510) 555-1234

THREE GOALS OF SOCIALIZATION

1. Teach your puppy to enjoy the presence, actions, and antics of all people — first the family, and then friends and strangers, especially children and men. Adult dogs tend to feel most uneasy around children and men, especially little boys. A dog's antipathy toward children and men is more likely to develop if the puppy grows up with few or none around, and if the puppy's social contacts with children and men have been unpleasant or scary.

2. Teach your puppy to enjoy being hugged and handled (restrained and examined) by people, especially by children, veterinarians, and groomers. Specifically, teach your puppy to enjoy being touched and handled in a variety of "hot spots," namely, around his collar, ears, paws, muzzle, tail, and rear end.

3. Teach your puppy to enjoy giving up valued objects when requested, especially her food bowl, bones, balls, chewtoys, garbage, and paper tissues.

1. TEACH YOUR PUPPY TO LIKE AND RESPECT PEOPLE

Compensate for your puppy's temporary but necessary social vacuum during her first month at home by introducing her to as many people as possible in the safety of her own home. Initial impressions are important, so make sure your puppy's first meetings with people are pleasant and enjoyable. Have every guest handfeed your puppy a couple of pieces of kibble. Puppies who enjoy the company of people grow up into adult dogs who enjoy the company of people. And dogs who enjoy the company of people are less likely to be frightened or bite.

Teaching your puppy to perform friendly, playful, and appeasing behaviors on cue helps people to feel good about your dog, and helps your dog to feel good about people.

Make sure to invite a number of different people to your home each day. It is not sufficient for your pup to meet the same people over and over again. Your puppy needs to grow accustomed to meeting strangers. Maintain routine hygiene at all times; have guests leave outdoor shoes outside and wash their hands before handling your puppy.

TRAINING TREATS

To prevent your puppy from pigging out on junk food treats, use your pup's daily ration of kibble as training treats. To prevent your puppy from being overfed by members of the family, measure your puppy's daily diet of kibble into a separate container first thing in the morning. Thus at any time of the day, if any kibble remains in the container, it may be fed to the puppy as a snack, as a meal, or individually handfed as rewards when training.

Give every guest a bag of training treats so that your puppy will be inclined to like people from the outset. Show your guests how you use your puppy's dinner kibble to lure/reward train him to Come, Sit, Lie down, using the technique described on pages 80–83. Ask your puppy to come. Praise it profusely as it approaches and give it a piece of kibble when it arrives. Back up and do it again.

In dog language, a play bow means "I am friendly and want to play," and raising a paw (shaking hands) means "I respect your higher rank and want to be friends."

Repeat the Come, Sit, and Down, sequence until the puppy responds reliably, and then help each guest practice these maneuvers until each one can get the puppy to come, sit, and lie down, three times in succession for a single piece of kibble.

When successfully lure/reward trained to come, sit, and lie down, your puppy dog demonstrates voluntary compliance and respect for your wishes, whether they are requests, instructions, or commands. There is absolutely no need to force or bully a dog to get him to show respect.

If your puppy is regularly handfed dinner by guests in this manner, he will soon learn to enjoy the company of people and to approach happily and sit automatically when greeting them. And, of course, as an added bonus you will have successfully trained your family and friends to help you train your puppy.

WILLING COMPLIANCE

- When a puppy dog approaches promptly and happily, it is a sure sign that he is people-friendly.

- Sitting and lying down in close proximity to people further shows that your dog likes them. Using food lures and rewards in training is the best possible way to teach your dog to like children and strangers.

- A puppy that has been taught by a range of people to lie down and roll over will have learned to show friendly appeasement and deference upon request.

- Most important, by coming, sitting, lying down, and rolling over on request, your dog shows respect for the person issuing instructions. This is especially important with children. When children lure/reward train, they issue commands, and the dog happily and voluntarily complies. And when it comes to dogs and children, happy and voluntary compliance is the only type of compliance that is effective and safe.

CHILDREN

The antics of children can be extremely scary to adult dogs who are not socialized with children during puppyhood. Even well-socialized adult dogs may get into trouble, since much that children do excites dogs and incites them to play and chase. Puppies and children must be taught how to behave around each other. This is easy and fun to do, so let's do it.

Even playful hugging may be scary for an unsocialized puppy and probably not tolerated by the dog in adulthood.

For puppy owners with children, the next few months present a bit of a challenge. It is infinitely worthwhile, however, because puppies successfully socialized with children generally develop exceedingly sound temperaments — they have to — and once they mature there is little in life that can surprise or upset them. However, to maximize the relationship between dogs and children and to ensure your dog's good nature and solid disposition, parents must educate their children as well as the pup. Teach your children how to act around the pup, and teach your pup how to act around children.

Puppy owners without children have a different kind of challenge. You must invite children to your home to meet your puppy now! However, unless your child-training skills exceed your puppy-training skills, initially invite over children only in small numbers. To start with, invite only a single child. One child is marvelous. Two are fine. But usually, three children plus a puppy quickly reach critical mass and emit levels of energy unmeasurable by any known scientific instrument. And, after all, we are trying to teach the puppy and the children to be calm and mannerly.

First, invite over only well-trained children. Supervise the children at all times. I repeat, supervise the children at all times. (Later on, puppy classes will offer a wonderful source of children who have been trained how to act around puppies and who have been trained how to train puppies.)

Children and puppies (or dogs) should never be left together unsupervised.

Second, invite over your friends' and relatives' children — children your puppy is likely to meet regularly or even occasionally as an adult.

With appropriate guidance and constant supervision, many children may become wonderful dog trainers.

Third, invite over neighborhood children. Remember, it is usually neighborhood kids who terrorize your dog through the garden fence, exciting him and inciting him to bark, growl, snap, and lunge. Then, of course, it is the children's parents, your neighbors, who complain because your dog is barking and harassing their kids. Dogs are less likely to bark at children they know and like, so give your puppy ample opportunity to get to know and like neighborhood children. Similarly, children are less likely to tease a dog they know and like owned by people they know and like, so give the neighborhood kids ample opportunity to get to know and like you and your puppy.

Give children tasty treats such as freeze-dried liver as well as kibble to use as lures and rewards during handling and training exercises. Thus, your puppy will quickly learn to love the presence, and presents, of children.

By coming when called and sitting on request, a puppy demonstrates willing compliance and shows respect to his trainer — a child.

For the first week, make sure your puppy's interactions with children are carefully controlled and calm. Thereafter, however, it is important for puppy parties to be festive. Balloons, streamers, and music set the stage, and treats for the puppies plus presents and noise-makers for the children set the scene.

It is so important that your puppy be very young when he first encounters and becomes thoroughly accustomed to the noise and activity of children. If your dog is already an adolescent before he sees his first child running and screaming in the park, generally you will be in for trouble because the dog will want to give chase.

However, for the lucky puppy who has hosted numerous puppy parties with children (or adults) laughing, screaming, running, skipping, and falling over... well, that's just old hat. Been there, done that! After just a couple of occasions partying with children, it is unlikely anything in real life will be as weird as what has become the snoring-boring, established status quo during puppy parties.

PUPPY PARTY GAMES

Initially, Round Robin Recalls and Puppy Push-ups are the best games to play. Have the children sit in chairs in a big circle. The first child calls the puppy and has him lie down and sit up three times in succession before sending him to the next child in the circle — "Rover, Go to Jamie," whereupon Jamie calls the puppy to come and perform three puppy push-ups, and so on. This is a wonderful exercise to practice prompt recalls and lightning-fast control commands — sits and downs.

In subsequent puppy parties, Biscuit Balance and Drop Dead Dog competitions are the name of the game. Give each child praise and a prize, but give special praise and special prizes to the children

Callahan learns Bang! — the command for a Down-Stay.

who can get the dog to balance a dog biscuit on his nose for the longest time — that is, the longest Sit-Stay — or can get the dog to lie doggo for the longest time — the longest Down-Stay.

Doug, a child at heart, teaches Skooter to balance a Milk-Bone on his head, and Skooter has fun learning a Sit-Stay.

As a rule of thumb, before your puppy is three months old he should have been handled and trained (to come, sit, lie down, and roll over) by at least twenty children.

MEN

Many adult dogs are more fearful of men than they are of women. So invite over as many men as possible to handle and gentle your puppy. It is especially important to invite men to socialize with

Chihuahua puppy cuddle time.

your puppy if no men are living in the household. Make sure you teach all male visitors how to handfeed kibble to lure/reward your pup to come, sit, lie down, and roll over. Add a few extra tasty treats to each male visitor's bag of training kibble so that your puppy forms a fond and loving bond with men.

STRANGERS

Young puppies tend to be universally accepting and tolerant of all people, but, unless taught otherwise, adolescent and adult dogs predictably develop a natural wariness of people they do not know. Introducing your puppy to a hundred people before he is three months old will help make him more accepting of strangers as an adolescent. To remain continually accepting of strangers, however, your adult dog needs to continually meet strangers. Meeting the same people over and over just won't do it. Your adult dog needs to meet new people each day, so you must maintain your newly improved social life at home or walk your dog regularly.

SIT TO SAY HELLO

As early as possible, establish sitting as the status quo for greeting people. Make sure each family member, visitor, or stranger has the puppy sit before they say hello, praise, pet, or offer a food reward. In no time, your puppy will learn to sit automatically when people approach. Sitting for praise or a food reward when greeting people certainly beats jumping up. And from the dog's viewpoint, sitting for attention, affection, and treats certainly beats getting punished for jumping up!

WARNING

If your puppy is slow to approach, or *doesn't* approach your guests, do something about it now. Certainly your puppy may be shy, but he is also undersocialized. It is absolutely abnormal for a two- to three-month-old puppy not to eagerly approach people. You must resolve this problem within one week. Otherwise, it will rapidly get worse — much worse. Moreover, if you let the days slip by, future attempts at therapeutic socialization will become progressively less effective. Please do not ignore your puppy's fears by rationalizing, "He takes a while to warm to strangers." If your pup takes a while to warm to strangers now, it will likely be intolerant and scared of strangers as an adult. It is simply not fair to let your puppy grow up to be scared and anxious around people. Please help your puppy today.

The solution is simple and effective, and usually only takes one week. For the next seven days, invite over half a dozen different people each day to handfeed your puppy's meals. For just one week, your puppy must not receive any food from family members or in his dog bowl. This technique works quickly if your puppy only receives kibble and treats from the hands of household guests. Once the puppy happily accepts food from the hand, your guests may then ask the pup to come, sit, and lie down for each piece of kibble. Your guests will soon become your puppy's new best friends.

A VERY IMPORTANT RULE

One single person can have a dramatic impact on your puppy's personality — for better or worse. Insist that nobody — *nobody* — interact or play with your puppy until they demonstrate they can get him to come eagerly, sit promptly, and lie down calmly.

Untrained visitors, especially children and adult male friends and relatives, are renowned for ruining good puppies in short order. If your visitors won't listen and wise up, put your puppy in his long-term confinement area, or ask the visitors to leave.

TEASING AND ROUGHHOUSING

Some people appear to enjoy teasing, manhandling, or roughhousing with puppies. Puppies may find teasing and roughhousing to be positive and enjoyable, or unpleasant and frightening.

Good-natured teasing can be a lot of fun for both parties. Properly done, teasing can do a lot to build a puppy's confidence by gradually and progressively desensitizing him to all the weird things people, especially men and children, do. On the other hand, relentless teasing can be frustrating and damaging. Malicious teasing is not teasing; it is abuse.

Confidence-building might involve temporarily withholding toys or treats from the pup, temporarily hugging or restraining the pup, making strange noises, or temporarily making mildly scary faces or slightly weird body movements, and then praising the pup and offering a food treat. The food reward builds the puppy's confidence by reinforcing his acceptance of your scary faces and weird actions. With each repetition you may act a little scarier and weirder before offering a treat. After time, your puppy will confidently accept any human action or mannerism. If the puppy ever refuses a treat, you have stressed it. So stop being silly for a while until you have handfed the pup half a dozen treats in a nonthreatening situation.

Puppies have to be trained to enjoy teasing. For example, being relentlessly pursued by a child with outstretched arms can be the scariest thing on the planet for a puppy without prior preparation. However, being pursued round the dining room table by an owner doing monster-walks can be one of the most enjoyable games for a puppy who has been taught to enjoy playing the game. Most dogs love to be chased as long as they have been taught that the game is nonthreatening.

Malicious teasing — taking pleasure in the puppy's displeasure — is just too cruel and silly for words. It is decidedly not funny to cause the puppy discomfort or to make him afraid. You are teaching the pup to distrust people, and it is your fault when, as an adult, the dog reacts defensively. Sadly though, it will be the dog who gets into trouble, not you. Please don't allow this to happen.

There is a simple test to determine whether or not the puppy finds teasing to be enjoyable. Stop the game, back up, and ask the

Roughhousing can be scary for puppies, and play-fighting is a common cause for owners' lack of control over their dogs. On the other hand, with just a little common sense, roughhousing and play-fighting can be the very best confidence-building, bite inhibition, and control exercises. Have frequent time-outs to calm, praise, and reassure your pup. Whenever your puppy's needle-sharp teeth cause pain, yelp! Ignore your puppy for thirty seconds or so and then instruct him to come, sit, and lie down before resuming play. Have frequent training interludes to check that you can still control your puppy and instantly get him to stop playing, to sit, lie down, and calm down.

puppy to come and sit. If the puppy comes promptly with a wagging tail and sits with his head held high, he is probably enjoying the game as much as you are. You may continue playing. If the pup approaches with a wiggly body, lowered head and tail, makes excessive licking motions with his tongue, and lies down or rolls over when asked to sit, you have pushed the puppy too far and he no longer trusts you. Stop playing and rebuild the puppy's confidence by repeatedly backing up and asking the pup to come and sit for a piece of kibble. If the puppy is slow to approach or doesn't come when called, he doesn't like you any more than he likes the evil game you're playing. Stop playing immediately. Take a long look in a mirror. Reflect on what you've done. Then go back and repair the damage by tossing food treats to the puppy until you can get him to confidently and happily come and sit three times in a row.

Because teasing may be beneficial or detrimental, you must regularly and repeatedly test that your puppy is having a good time. Check that the pup will come and sit before starting the game, and stop the game at least every fifteen seconds to see if he will still do so. This is a sensible precaution anyway, to check that you are still in control of the puppy, even when he is excited and having fun.

Similarly, make sure that your family and friends all demonstrate the same ability to get the pup to come, sit, lie down, and roll over before allowing them to play with your puppy. This simple and effective precaution should apply to men, women, and children.

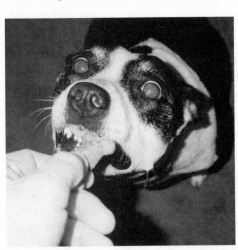

When played intelligently, physical games, such as play-fighting and tug-o'-war, are effective bite inhibition and control exercises, and are wonderful for motivating adult dogs during obedience training. In order to be effective and not produce out-of-control dogs, however, these games must be played according to strict rules, the most important being that you are in control at all times. That is, at any time you are able to get your puppy to stop playing and lie down calmly with a single down command. If you do not have this level of control, do not roughhouse with your puppy. If, on the other hand, you would like to play physical games with your puppy, I suggest you read my booklet on *Preventing Aggression Behavior,* again available from James & Kenneth Publishers.

HANDFEEDING

1. Handfeeding teaches your puppy to like kibble. Kibble may then be used effectively as lures and rewards for handling and gentling exercises and for basic training, especially by children, men, and strangers.

2. Handfeeding teaches your puppy to like training and her trainers, especially children, men, and strangers.

3. Teaching your puppy "Off" and "Take it" will help prevent her from becoming a food guarder.

4. Teaching your puppy to "Take it...Gently" is the very core of your puppy's developing a soft mouth and learning bite inhibition.

5. Handfeeding enables you to choose convenient times for teaching your pup to control her jaws, rather than having to deal with your puppy whenever she decides to play-bite and bother you.

2. HANDLING AND GENTLING

Living with and loving a dog you cannot touch, cuddle, or hug is just about as silly as living with and loving a person you cannot hug. It is also potentially dangerous. Even so, veterinarians and groomers will tell you that hard-to-handle dogs are extremely common. Indeed, many dogs are extremely stressed when restrained and/or examined by strangers. There are few physical differences between hugging and restraint, or between handling and examination. The difference depends on your puppy's perspective. Generally, puppies feel they are hugged and handled by friends, but restrained and examined by strangers.

What's the point of living with a dog if he doesn't like being handled or hugged?

Veterinarians and groomers simply cannot do their jobs unless your dog remains relaxed and still while being examined. Fearful and aggressive adult dogs and sometimes just plain wriggly adolescent dogs often need to be restrained, tranquilized, or even anesthetized for routine physical examination, teeth-cleaning, and grooming. Restraint makes the procedure much scarier for dogs. Untrained dogs are exposed to the risk of anesthesia, the additional safety precautions consume the veterinarian's time, and hence the owners must pay more money. It is just too silly. Adult humans do not require anesthesia during routine trips to the doctor, dentist, and hairdresser; neither would dogs, if only their owners had taught them to enjoy meeting and being handled by people.

It is simply not fair to allow your puppy to grow up to be wary and anxious around people and afraid of their touch. It is cruel to invite an ultra-social animal to live in the world of humans, yet neglect to teach him to enjoy human company and contact. The poor dog is subjected to a lifetime of psychological torture, which in many ways is worse than other kinds of abuse.

It is not sufficient that your pup merely tolerates handling; he must learn to thoroughly enjoy being handled by strangers. A dog who doesn't thoroughly enjoy being restrained and examined by strangers is a time bomb waiting to go off. One day an unfamiliar child will attempt to hug and pet your dog. Your dog may object. Then the child, you, and your dog all have a big problem.

Your puppy needs to be handled by familiar people before unfamiliar people, adults before children, women before men, and girls before boys.

As with the socialization exercises, adult family members need to accustom the pup to enjoy being handled and gently restrained first. Then your puppy knows and enjoys the handling and gentling game before strangers and children become involved. It is quite easy — and thoroughly enjoyable — to teach young puppies to like being handled and examined by people, whereas teaching adolescent and adult dogs to accept handling, especially by children and strangers, can be time-consuming and potentially dangerous. So do not delay. Do it now.

HUGGING / RESTRAINT

This is the fun part: you get to hug your puppy. In fact every family member and all your guests get to hug the puppy. Relaxing with your puppy is a lot of fun, especially if your puppy is relaxed. If he is not relaxed, you are going to teach your puppy to relax, calm down, and thoroughly enjoy a good long cuddle.

Provided your pup was handled frequently prior to weaning, and especially neonatally, at eight weeks of age it should go as limp as a noodle whenever picked up, and should settle down as relaxed as a rag doll on your lap. Even if your puppy did not have the benefit of plentiful early handling in his original home, handling exercises are easy at eight weeks of age. However, you had better get started, because in just twelve weeks' time, with a hard-to-handle five-month-old adolescent, the same simple handling exercises will be a completely different story. Untrained adolescent dogs are notoriously difficult to handle.

Before starting specific handling exercises, make sure that your puppy is perfectly relaxed lying in your lap. Once your puppy trusts you and has developed sufficient confidence, he will happily snuggle and flop as loose as a rag doll.

Pick up your pup, put him on your lap, and hook one finger around his collar so that he doesn't jump off. Slowly and repetitively stroke the pup along the top of his head and back in an attempt to get him to settle down in any position he finds comfortable. If your pup is a bit squirrelly and squirmy, soothingly massage his chest or the base of his ears. Once the pup is completely relaxed, pick up the pup and lay him down on his back for a soothing tummy rub. Massage his belly by making a repetitive circular motion with the palm of your hand. Gently rubbing the pup's inguinal area (where the inside of the thigh joins the abdomen) will also help the puppy relax. While your puppy is calm and relaxed, periodically pick him up to give him a short hug. Gradually and progressively increase the length of the hugs (restraint). After a while, pass the puppy to someone else and have them repeat the above exercises.

CALMING QUICKLY

In addition to lengthy periods of massage and occasional hugs, see how quickly you can get your pup to calm down. Alternate short play sessions with periods of calming down and gentle restraint. Once the puppy calms down quickly in your lap, try getting him to calm down on the floor.

TANTRUMS

Should your pup struggle violently, or especially if he has a tantrum, *you must not let go*. Otherwise your puppy will learn that if he struggles or throws a tantrum, he needn't calm down and be handled because the owner gives in. Bad news! With one hand on your pup's collar and the palm of your other hand against the puppy's chest, gently but firmly hold the pup's back against your abdomen. Hold the puppy so that his four legs point away from you and sufficiently low down against your abdomen so that he cannot turn his head and bite your face. Hold the pup until he calms down, which he will eventually do. Continue massaging the pup's ear with the fingers of one hand and his chest with the fingertips of your other hand. As soon as the puppy calms down and stops struggling, praise the pup, and after a few seconds of calm let him go. Then repeat the procedure.

If you have difficulty getting the pup to calm down and enjoy being hugged (restrained) after one day of practice, call a trainer to your home immediately. This is an emergency. You do not want to live with a dog you cannot handle or hug. Call the Association of Pet Dog Trainers at 1-800-PET-DOGS to locate a Certified Pet Dog Trainer (CPDT) in your area.

ALPHA ROLLOVER???

As I mentioned before, your puppy will not trust and respect you if manhandled and forcibly restrained on his back. It will become more resistant. You'll soon have a puppy that doesn't even enjoy being cuddled because he perceives your hugs as forcible restraint. Be gentle and patient as described above.

HANDLING / EXAMINATION

Teaching your eight-week-old puppy to enjoy being handled and examined is as easy as it is essential. Moreover, your pup's veterinarian, trainer, and groomer will be forever grateful, as will be you and your puppy. It is a truly unfortunate puppy that finds it scary to be handled and examined.

Many dogs have a number of "hot spots," which if not defused in puppyhood can be extremely sensitive to touch. Handling the ears, paws, muzzle, collar area, and rear end often provokes a defensive reaction in an adult dog if these areas have not been desensitized during puppyhood. Similarly, an adult dog may act fearfully or defensively when you stare into his eyes if as a puppy he was not taught to enjoy direct eye contact.

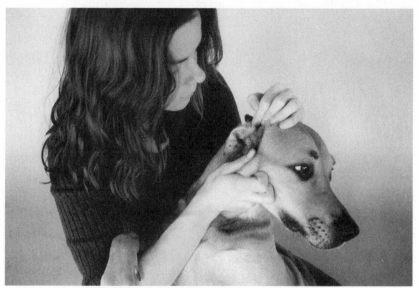

Make sure your puppy feels totally at ease when you handle and examine his ears, muzzle, teeth, and paws. Handfeed your puppy a lot of kibble as you examine each specific area.

Some areas become sensitive over time simply because nobody
bothers to examine them. For example, few owners regularly inspect
their dog's rear end, or open his mouth to examine the teeth. Some
areas are naturally sensitive and may provoke a reaction even in puppies. For example, nearly every puppy will bite your hand if you
firmly take hold of his leg or paw. Other areas become sensitive
because of bad husbandry and mishandling. Dogs with hangy-down
ears, which are prone to infection, soon come to associate ear exam-
inations with pain. Similarly, many adult dogs associate being stared
at or being grabbed by the collar with bad times. Dogs quickly
become hand-shy when people take them by the collar to lead
them to confinement, grab them by the collar to put them on leash
(ending an otherwise enjoyable play session in the park), or grab
them by the collar to punish them for some transgression.

Handling and examination exercises serve to defuse the hot
spots and help the puppy form positive associations with being

*Please remember that your puppy has two ears and four paws! Many
veterinarians and groomers get quite a shock examining the second ear or
the hind paws if the owner has practiced handling only one ear (usually
the dog's left ear with the right hand) and only the front paws.*

handled. Desensitizing the puppy and teaching him to enjoy handling is simple when combined with handfeeding him kibble. It is so simple, in fact, that it is surprising there are so many hard-to-handle adult dogs.

Use your puppy's daily allotment of kibble as training treats. Take hold of your pup's collar and offer a treat. Gaze into your pup's eyes and offer a treat. Look in one ear and offer a treat. Look in the other ear and offer another treat. Hold a paw and offer a treat. Repeat with each paw. Open his mouth and offer a treat. Feel his rear end and private parts and offer a treat. And then repeat the sequence. Each time you repeat the process, progressively handle and examine each area more thoroughly and for longer periods.

Once your puppy is quite happy being handled and examined by family members, it is time to play Pass the Puppy with your guests. One at a time, have each guest offer the pup a treat, take hold of his collar, look in his eyes, handle and examine his ears, paws, teeth, and rear end, and offer treats as described above before passing the pup (plus the bag of dinner kibble) to the next person.

Few people intend to hurt or frighten a puppy, but accidents happen. For example, a guest may inadvertently step on his paw, or the owner might accidentally grab his hair when reaching for the collar. But if the pup feels secure when being handled, he will be less likely to react defensively.

TWO UNDENIABLE FACTS ABOUT PUNISHMENT

1. Any punishment for inappropriate behavior is an advertisement that you have yet to effectively teach your dog how you would like him to act.

2. In most cases, the dog associates punishment with the trainer and the training situation, understandably causing him to dislike both training and the trainer.

PUNISHMENT

Insufficient socialization and frequent and extreme punishment are the two major reasons dogs become wary of people. Wary dogs stay away from people. Problems happen when people approach and try to handle, or pet, the dog.

Few people intend to make things unpleasant for their puppy dog, with one notable exception: when punishing him. By definition, punishment is meant to be unpleasant. However, it is extremely disturbing that this unpleasantness is overly frequent and overly extreme. Sadly, many outdated trainers, and hence many owners who have read outdated training books, tend to focus on punishing untrained dogs for getting it wrong, for breaking rules they never knew existed. It is much quicker to teach your puppy the rules of the house — to show him what you want him to do and to reward him for doing it. Thus, your puppy learns to *want* to do what you want him to do. Frequent or extreme punishment is a major reason why many dogs dislike being handled, and why they dislike the handler.

Frequent punishment is an indication that your training philosophy is flawed. The dog still frequently misbehaves and, therefore, is frequently punished. Training is simply not working. Time to change to Plan B. Rather than punishing your puppy for mistakes he has made in the past, you should concentrate on teaching your puppy how he should act in the future. Remember, it is much more efficient and effective to reward your puppy for doing it your way — the one way you consider to be right — rather than trying to punish him for the many ways he could do it wrong.

Repeated punishment is the painful tip of a wedge that progressively divides and destroys the pet–owner relationship. Initially, you will lose off-leash control, your dog will be slow to approach since he no longer wants to come close. Eventually he will become wary and apprehensive when approached and handled. The whole point of living with a dog is to enjoy his company.

Surely you don't want to live with a dog who doesn't want your companionship. If you find yourself frequently reprimanding and punishing your puppy, seek help from a trainer.

Extreme punishment is an extreme indication that training isn't working. The dog still misbehaves and the severity of punishment is increased with the assumption that it will be more effective. If punishment is effective, the dog would no longer misbehave. If the dog continues to misbehave following an extreme punishment, it would be wise to question the validity of the punishment-training program rather than automatically upping the level of pain.

Extreme punishment is quite unnecessary and absolutely counterproductive. It creates more problems than it resolves. Even when extreme punishment eliminates an unwanted behavior, it trashes the dog-human relationship. For example, your puppy may not jump up anymore following a severe punishment, but now he no longer likes you, nor wants to come close to you because you were extremely nasty to him the last time he jumped up to say hello. You have won the battle but lost the war. Your dog doesn't jump up, but you don't have a best friend anymore. Sadly, training has become adversarial and unpleasant. Why would a person treat their best friend like their worst enemy?

If you ever feel the need to resort to severe punishment, immediately seek help from a trainer who uses more efficient and effective, dog-friendly, lure/reward training methods. The most successful obedience competition dogs, agility dogs, search and rescue dogs, bomb detection dogs, seeing-eye dogs, hearing-ear dogs, assistance dogs, and protection dogs are all trained using reward-based motivational methods, with few — if any — reprimands. Isn't it about time that we trained pet dogs the same way?

When effectively using reward-training techniques, punishment is seldom necessary. However, a less-experienced trainer may feel the need to reprimand or punish more frequently in order to compensate for novice training skills. Even so, when punishing a dog there is no need to approach, loom over, glower, grab, shake, shout, scream, scare, or hurt her.

For a routine training mishap, an instructive reprimand is more than sufficient, such as, "Outside!" "Chewtoy!" "Sit!" "Steady!" or "Hustle!" The slightly raised voice and change in tone indicates urgency, and in each case, the one-word instruction lets your puppy know what she should be doing to get back on track again.

Even for more serious transgressions, harsh punishment is unnecessary. In fact, when you use fun and games, reward-based training methods, banishment is the all-time most effective punishment — a short time-out with no more training game, no more rewards, and no more *you*. Calmly and quietly instruct your dog to leave the room: "Rover, Exit!" Banishment need only last for one or two minutes. Then always insist that the dog apologize and make up by dutifully coming, sitting, and lying down. When banishment becomes your best punishment, you have achieved the Holy Grail of Dog Training.

Banishment is especially effective if you cheerfully shake the dog's treat jar during the time-out period. When one of my dogs is in a time-out penalty, I make a point of merrily training my other dog and especially giving out lots of "bad-dog treats." "Good dog, Oso! Why don't you have one of bad-dog-Phoenie's treats?" It works well in our household. On one occasion, I became so irritated that Phoenix was ignoring me that during her time-out from the living room I pretended to eat the treats myself. "Mmmmm! Yummy-yummy Phoenie's treats!" When I let her back in the living room, she lay down and wouldn't take her eyes off of me for half an hour.

Giving the banishment order in a soft, sweet voice and pointing demonstratively to the door will help control your upset and emotions. On the first couple of occasions, you may have to shoo your puppy through the door, but it will soon learn to leave promptly following your command. Moreover, after just a few banishments, your soft and sweet "Exit!" command will become a conditioned punishment, having an immediate and dramatic effect on your pup's behavior. At this stage in training, the "Exit!" command becomes an extremely effective warning. Observe your puppy's reaction when you sweetly inquire, "Rover, would you like to pay attention and take heed, or would you prefer to Exit?" Most likely, your pup will wise up immediately. If so, ask her to lie down quietly and let her stay beside you. If not, say "Exit!" in your best sweet and soft voice and demonstratively point to the door.

When banished, most dogs leave reluctantly and remain right outside the door looking in. However, when working with young puppies without much training, it is better for you to leave promptly when the puppy misbehaves. In that case, play/train in your pup's long-term confinement area so that during her time-out your pup does not have the opportunity to get into further mischief. A one- or two-minute time-out is sufficient. Then return to the puppy's area and ask her to make up and show some respect by coming, sitting, and lying down on request.

GRABITIS

Twenty percent of dog bites occur when a family member reaches to grab the dog by the scruff or collar. One doesn't need to be a rocket scientist to figure this out. Obviously, the dog has learned that when people grab him by the collar bad things often happen. Consequently, the dog becomes hand-shy, plays Catch-Me-If-You-Can, or reacts defensively. It is potentially dangerous to have a dog dodge you when you reach for his collar. For example, you need to know you could effectively grab your dog if he ever tried to dash out the front door.

So teach your puppy to enjoy being grabbed by the collar. First, prevent your pup from forming negative associations to human hands, and second, teach your pup that being taken by the collar has only positive consequences.

1. If you let your puppy play without interruption, and then take him by the collar to end the play session, of course he will come to dislike your reaching for his collar because a collar grab signals the end of the play session. Starting in the house and later in the park, frequently interrupt puppy play sessions by taking your puppy by the collar, asking him to sit, praising him, offering a piece of kibble, and then letting him go play again. The puppy thus learns that being taken by the collar is not necessarily the end of the play session. Instead, a collar grab is a short time-out for refreshment and a few kind words from his owner before the puppy gets to play again. Also, interrupting play allows you to use resumption of play to reward your puppy for sitting and allowing you to take him by the collar.

2. If you lead or drag your puppy into confinement, he will no doubt come to dislike being taken by the collar, as he will come to dislike confinement. Instead, teach your puppy to enjoy confinement. Stuff a bunch of hollow chewtoys with kibble and put them in your puppy's confinement area, and then close the door with your puppy on the outside. In no time at all, your puppy will beg to go inside. Now simply instruct your pup, "Go to your bed (or crate)" or "Go to your playroom (long-term confinement area)," and open the door. Your pup will happily rush inside and settle down peacefully with his chewtoys.

3. Above all, promise your puppy that you will never *(never)* call your puppy and then grab him by the collar to reprimand or punish. Doing this just once will make him hate coming when called and hate when you reach for his collar. If you punish your puppy after he comes to you, he will take longer to come the next time. Eventually slow recalls will become no recalls. Your puppy will still

misbehave; only now you will be unable to catch him! If you ever punish your puppy after taking his collar, he will soon become hand-shy, evasive, and defensive.

To prevent your puppy from becoming hand-shy, take hold of his collar and then offer a piece of kibble. Repeat this procedure many times throughout the day, and with each successive trial progressively increase the speed with which you reach for the collar. Your puppy will soon develop a strong positive association with being grabbed and may even look forward to it.

If your puppy is already even a tiny bit hand-shy, the last thing you want to do is reach for his collar. Instead, practice reaching for and handling areas he does not mind having touched or actually enjoys having touched. Then, gradually and progressively work toward the collar. Using kibble as a training treat, start by offering the dog a treat to let him know the game's afoot. "Not a bad start," thinks the dog. Then touch the tip of his tail and immediately offer another treat for his trouble. Trouble? "No trouble," thinks the dog. If it is possible to touch the tip of the tail, then surely it is possible to touch just one inch down from the tip. Give the dog another treat and touch two inches down, then three inches down, and so on. On each repetition, touch the dog a little closer to his collar. It is only a matter of time before you can reach for and handle the dog's collar without upsetting the dog. When touching the dog's collar the first couple of times, offer one or two pieces of freeze-dried liver.

The key to progressive desensitization is to work slowly. If you even suspect the dog is a little intimidated or uneasy, go right back to square one — in this case, the tip of the tail — and this time work slower.

"I ATE MY DOG'S HOMEWORK" AND OTHER COMMON EXCUSES FOR NOT SOCIALIZING YOUR PUPPY

"He's fine with me."

Wonderful! Certainly the first step of socialization is to make sure the puppy is perfectly friendly with the family. But it is imperative that the pup become Mr. Sociable with friends, neighbors, visitors, and strangers so that he does not object to being examined by the veterinarian or playfully grabbed and hugged by children.

"We have a big family. Our puppy gets more than enough socialization."

Not true! In order to be accepting of strangers as an adult, your puppy needs to meet at least three unfamiliar people each day, not the same people over and over again.

"I don't have any friends to help me socialize my puppy."

Well, you soon will. Socializing your puppy will do wonders for *your* social life. Invite your neighbors over to meet the pup. Invite people over from work. Check out the puppy classes in your area and invite over some puppy owners from there. They will more than appreciate the problems you are about to encounter in the future.

If you cannot get people to come to your home to meet the puppy, take her to safe places to meet people. Do not put her on the ground in public places that may have been frequented by unvaccinated adult dogs until she is at least three months old and current with her vaccinations. Buy a soft carrier and take your puppy on errands, for example, to the bank, the bookstore, or hardware store. See if you can take your puppy to work. Later on, you will be able to take your pup to puppy classes, to dog parks, and on neighborhood walks. But she needs to meet lots of people right away. So whatever you do, do not keep your puppy a secret.

"I don't want my dogs to accept food treats from strangers."

Perhaps your concern is that someone may poison the dog. As a rule, dogs are only poisoned when left alone in backyards — because they are not housetrained and therefore cannot be left safely indoors — or when let loose to range and roam. But you are not inviting dog-hating strangers to interact with your puppy. Instead, you are inviting over selected family, neighbors, and friends. Regardless, every puppy should be taught never to touch or take any object, including food, from any person's hand unless first the puppy hears, "Rover, Take it," or some such command. Having learned these basic manners, your dog will only accept food from people who know his name and who know the appropriate take it command — namely, from family and friends.

"I don't want my dog to like strangers. I want him to protect me."

Try telling that to your veterinarian or to your children's friends' parents. However, if you mean you want your dog to perform some protective function, that's a different matter. But surely you are not going to leave it up to a poorly socialized dog to make decisions regarding whom to protect, whom to protect against, and how to protect. Any good protection dog has first been super-socialized to the point of total confidence, and then carefully taught how, when, and whom to protect.

Training your dog to bark or growl on command is a more than sufficient protective deterrent. Your dog may be taught to vocalize in certain situations: for example, when somebody steps onto your property or touches your car. Alarm barkers are extremely effective deterrents, especially if they do not bark when people simply walk by your house or car.

"I don't have the time."

Then give the puppy to someone who does have the time! This puppy may still be saved if someone is willing to take the time to socialize it.

"I need to alpha roll and dominate my pup to get it to respect me."

Not necessarily. Or, not at all. If you physically force and dominate your puppy, he won't respect you. He may heed your commands — grudgingly and fearfully — but he certainly won't respect you. More likely, your dog will grow to resent you.

Besides, there are easy and enjoyable ways to get your dog to show respect. Years ago in one of my puppy classes, I remember a young couple who had a four-year-old daughter named Kristen and a Rottweiler named Panzer. In class, Kristen had the dog better trained than her parents and could consistently get Panzer to come, sit, lie down, and roll over. Kristen would give Panzer a tummy rub when he was lying on his side and he would raise his hind leg to expose his belly. Kristen would talk to Panzer in a squeaky little voice. Kristin squeaked and Panzer did it. Or, we could say that Kristen requested and Panzer agreed. Or, that Kristen commanded and Panzer obeyed. More important, though, Panzer happily and willingly complied. And when it comes to children training dogs, happy willing compliance is the only kind of compliance that is safe and makes sense.

Was Kristen dominating Panzer? Absolutely! But in a much more effective way than by using brute force. As a child, Kristen had to use brain instead of brawn to control Panzer's behavior. Kristen mentally dominated Panzer's will.

Kristen's training engendered Panzer's respect and friendship. Panzer respected her wishes. Also, by approaching promptly off-leash, Panzer demonstrated that he liked Kristen. By sitting and lying down, Panzer showed that he really liked Kristen and wanted to stay close to her. By rolling over, Panzer displayed appeasement.

And by lifting his leg to expose his inguinal area, Panzer displayed deference. In doggy language, exposing the inguinal region means, "I am a lowly worm. I respect your higher rank, and I would like to be friends."

If you want your puppy to respect you, lure/reward train him to come, sit, lie down, and roll over. If you want your puppy to show deference, teach him to lick your hand or shake hands. Licking and pawing are both active appeasement gestures — signs of wanting to be friends. If you would like your puppy to show doggy deference, tickle his goolies when he is lying on his side and watch him raise his hind leg to expose his inguinal area.

"Dogs of this breed are particularly hard to handle."

Using this excuse to give up on handling, gentling, and socialization exercises is too silly for words. If your research on dog breeds has convinced you that you truly have a difficult breed, you should double or triple the socialization and handling exercises, wind back all developmental deadlines, and start each batch of exercises earlier. Strangely enough, though, I have heard this excuse given for just about every breed of dog. As soon as you think that your chosen breed is too much dog for you, seek help immediately. Find a trainer who can teach you how to handle your puppy before you cause irreparable damage to his temperament.

"My spouse/significant other/parent/child/living companion selected the most dominant pup in the litter."

Did you remember the cardinal rule of puppy selection, that all family members completely agree? Well, it's a bit late for that now, and so I would suggest the same advice as above. As soon as you suspect you have a difficult pup, double or triple the socialization and handling exercises and start each batch of exercises earlier. Additionally, you might consider learning how to train your spouse, significant other, parent, child, or living companion.

"Something is genetically wrong with the puppy."

Same advice as above: as soon as you suspect your puppy has some kind of organic problem, double or triple the socialization and handling exercises and start each batch of exercises earlier.

It's a bit late for genetic screening, and, in any case, what else can you do — tweak the dog's genes? Many people use breed, dominance, or organic conditions as an excuse to give up on the pup — and as an excuse to not socialize and train him. In reality, socialization and training are the puppy's only hope. Your puppy needs socialization and training. Lots of it! Right away!

Regardless of breed and breeding, and regardless of your puppy's socialization and training prior to coming to your home, as of right now any change in your puppy's temperament, behavior, or manners is completely dependent on how you socialize and train it. Work with your puppy and it will get better. Don't work with your puppy and it will get worse. Your puppy's future is entirely in your hands.

"He's just a puppy!" or *"He's soooo cute!"* or *"He's only playing!"* or *"He'll grow out of it!"*

Of course your puppy is only playing — play-barking, play-growling, play-biting, play-fighting, play-protecting a bone, or playing tug-o'-war. If you just laugh at him, your pup will continue playing the aggression game as he grows older, and, in no time at all, your fully grown adult dog will be playing for real.

Puppy play is all important. Play is essential if a puppy is to learn the social relevance of the vast jumble of behaviors in his doggy repertoire, specifically the appropriateness and inappropriateness of each behavior in each setting. In a sense, play enables a pup to learn what he can get away with. What you need to do is teach your puppy the rules of the game. And the more rules he learns in puppyhood, the safer he will be as an adult dog.

Puppy barking and growling are quite normal and acceptable, just as long as you can stop the noise when you wish. Stopping an eight-week-old puppy from barking or growling is pretty easy. Be still yourself, so the puppy may calm down more easily. Say, "Puppy, Shush!" and waggle a food treat in front of its nose. Say, "Good dog," and offer the treat when the pup eventually shushes. Similarly, tug-o'-war is a normal and acceptable game, just as long as your pup never initiates the game and you can get the pup to release the object and sit at any time. Both are easy rules to teach to an eight-week-old puppy. When playing tug-o'-war, instruct your puppy to release the object and sit at least every fifteen seconds. Periodically stop tugging, say, "Thank you," and waggle a food treat in front of its nose. When the puppy releases the object to sniff the treat, praise him, and ask him to sit. When he sits, praise him profusely, offer the food treat, and then resume the game.

Later sections offer guidelines for the object-guarding game, play-biting, and play-fighting.

BARKING AND GROWLING ON CUE

A puppy can easily be trained to bark and growl on command, which has many practical uses. Tell him, "Speak!" Then have someone ring the doorbell to prompt the pup to bark. After several repetitions, your puppy will bark when you say, "Speak!" in anticipation of the doorbell. Your pup can similarly be taught to growl on command. While playing tug-o'-war, ask your pup to growl and tug vigorously on the toy. When he growls, praise him enthusiastically. Then say, "Puppy, Shush!" Stop tugging and let him sniff the food treat. When the pup stops growling, praise him calmly, and offer the food treat.

Teaching your puppy to bark and growl on cue facilitates teaching "Shush!" Requesting your pup to vocalize allows you to teach it "Shush!" at your convenience. This is much easier than trying to quiet the pup when it is over-the-top with excitement when someone is at the front door or afraid of an approaching stranger. Alternate "Speak!" and "Shush!" until your pup has it

perfect. He will soon learn to shush at times when he is obediently barking or growling. Now your puppy will understand when
you ask him to be quiet when he is excited or afraid.

*Training a dog to bark and growl on command inspires confidence in both
dog and owner. Teaching barking and growling on cue also facilitates
teaching "Shush!"*

A noisy dog tends to frighten people more than a quiet dog,
especially a dog who barks repetitively and works himself into a
frenzy. A simple, well-trained "Shush!" request will quickly quiet
and calm the dog and make him less scary to visitors and especially
children.

Teaching "Shush!" is only fair to your dog. So many dogs are
repeatedly reprimanded and punished for barking and growling
simply because no one has taught them to shush on command.
The sad thing is that many adult dogs bark only out of excitement, enthusiasm, or boredom. Or they bark and growl as a solici-
tation to play the same games they played with you when they
were puppies.

EUPHEMISM, LITOTES, AND OTHER OUTRAGEOUS SILLINESS!

"She takes a while to warm to strangers!" "He's not overly fond of children!" and "He's a bit hand-shy!"

How can anyone live with a dog knowing that he is stressed by the presence of strangers and children and scared of human hands? The poor dog must be in a state of extreme anxiety. Just how many times does this dog have to beg, implore, and warn you that he feels uncomfortable around strangers and children and doesn't like people reaching for his collar? This is simply an accident waiting to happen. What if an unfamiliar child should reach for the dog's collar, possibly around the dog's food bowl, when the dog is having a bad-hair day and not feeling good? A dog bite for sure. What will we say? That the dog bit without warning and without reason? The poor dog had at least five good reasons to bite: (1) a stranger, (2) a child, (3) reaching for his collar, (4) proximity to his food bowl, and (5) not feeling good. And the dog has been warning his family repeatedly for some time.

If there is anything that upsets your puppy, desensitize him to that specific stimulus or scenario immediately. Help your puppy build his confidence so that he may approach everyday events without stress or fear. The required confidence-building exercises have all been described. Use them!

3. GUARDING VALUED OBJECTS

Object-guarding, a common problem with family dogs, will develop throughout puppyhood if owners allow it to. Owners may

fail to notice their adolescent dog becoming increasingly possessive and protective. Some may actually encourage their puppy's
protective displays, thinking they are cute.

It is natural for dogs to protect their possessions. In the wild, a
wolf would hardly pop next door to borrow a cup of bones. Domestic dogs quickly learn that once something is gone, it is gone. So it is
not surprising to find dogs trying to keep their possessions away from
people.

Bitches are more likely to guard objects than male dogs. In a
domestic pack, it is fairly common to see a very low-ranking bitch
successfully defend her bone from a relatively high-ranking male
dog. In fact, The Bitch's First Amendment to Male Hierarchical
Rule is "I have it, and you don't!" With male dogs, nothing better
advertises insecurity and lack of confidence than object-guarding.
Object-guarding is common with middle-ranking, insecure male
dogs. It is definitely not "top dog behavior." In fact, true top dogs
are confident in their position and usually quite willing to share a
bone, toy, or food bowl with lower-ranking individuals.

If you frequently take food or toys away from your puppy and
she never gets them back, your pup will learn that relinquishing an
object likely means she will never see it again. Understandably,
your pup might develop behaviors to keep objects away from you.
She may run and hide with the object, hold on tight with her
jaws, growl, snarl, and maybe snap.

If you find you are backing down when your puppy is protect-
ing any object, and are at a loss for what to do, seek help from a
pet dog trainer immediately. This problem will quickly get out of
hand, and soon you will have an *adult* dog backing you down.
Retraining adult dogs who are protective of valued objects is complicated, time-consuming, and not without danger. You will definitely require assistance from an experienced trainer or behavior
counselor. On the other hand, preventing this in puppyhood is
easy and safe.

You can easily teach your puppy "Off" and "Take it" when handfeeding kibble. Say, "Take it," and handfeed a piece of kibble. Repeat this three more times. Then say, "Off," and present the kibble firmly hidden in your fist. Let the puppy worry at your fist for as long as you like. The puppy will paw and mouth your hand. (Of course, if the puppy's teeth cause pain, yelp! Ignore your puppy for a thirty-second time-out, and then instruct the pup to come, sit, and lie down before proceeding with the exercise.) Eventually, your pup will temporarily give up and withdraw her muzzle. As soon as the pup relinquishes contact with your hand, say, "Take it," and open your hand so that the puppy may take the kibble from your palm. Repeat the sequence over and over, progressively increasing the requisite length of noncontact before you instruct your pup to take the kibble each time. I find it helps to praise the puppy for non-contact by counting "good dogs": "Good Dog One, Good Dog Two, Good Dog Three," and so on. Once your puppy has learned not to touch your hand for a count of ten "good dogs," you may present the kibble between finger and thumb when instructing, "Off." Eventually, you may practice saying, "Off," and placing the kibble on the floor and then picking it up again before saying, "Take it."

First make sure that your puppy develops a strong chewtoy habit. If she always wants to play with her chewtoys, she won't seek out inappropriate objects that need to be taken away. Additionally, teach your pup to voluntarily relinquish her chewtoys on request.

Basically, you have to teach your puppy that voluntarily

relinquishing an object does not mean losing it for good. Your puppy should learn that giving up bones, toys, and tissues means receiving something better in return — praise and treats — and also later getting back the original object.

Teaching "Off" has many useful applications.

THE TOKEN SYSTEM — EXCHANGING VALUED COMMODITIES FOR TREATS

Start working with objects that both you and your puppy can hold at the same time, such as a rolled newspaper or a Kong on a rope. Physical contact is a very big part of the possession game. Your puppy is less likely to protect an object if you still have hold of it. However, as soon as you let go, your pup becomes more likely to defend her prize.

As practiced in the previous exercise, tell your puppy "Off" and then "Take it." Waggle the object in front of her muzzle enticingly. Praise your puppy when she takes hold. Do not let go of the object. Say, "Puppy, Thank you," stop waggling the object to encourage your puppy to stop tugging, and with your other hand, waggle a very tasty treat (freeze-dried liver) in front of her nose. Praise your puppy as soon as she opens her mouth and you have regained full possession of the object. Continue praising as you offer one, two, or three treats, maybe luring the puppy to sit or lie down as you do so. Then instruct your pup to take the object again and repeat the procedure. When your puppy has promptly relinquished the object upon request five times in a row, you may let go of the object each time. Now you are ready to work with smaller objects, such as a Kong without a rope, tennis balls, Biscuit Balls, sterilized bones, or other toys. Once your pup eagerly takes and gives promptly, simply drop or toss the object and say, "Thank you." Voilà! Your very own faithful retriever pup!

Retrieving is a lot of fun and good exercise. It has numerous applications, such as looking for lost keys, fetching slippers, and clearing up dog toys. Most puppies love retrieving and quickly develop confidence about surrendering objects. Puppies think it's a great deal. They temporarily swap their toys for treats, the owner safely holds the toy while they enjoy the treat, and then they get the toy back to exchange for more treats.

In fact, some puppies enjoy proffering objects so much that it may become a bother to the owner. If your pup offers too many unsolicited presents, simply instruct her, "Take it to your bed." In fact, this is one of the best ways to teach your puppy to clear up her toys.

By teaching your puppy to retrieve objects, what had intrinsic value as a toy now has additional value as a token that may be exchanged for praise and reward. Playing fetch with your puppy is a wonderful way to supercharge her toys, increase their effectiveness as lures and rewards for training, and greatly increase the likelihood that a bored puppy will seek out her toys to play with rather than inappropriate household or outdoor articles.

Once the above exchange exercises are working, increase the intrinsic value of the objects by stuffing the Kong or sterilized bone with treats. Before your puppy is ten weeks old, you should also repeat the following confidence-building exercises many times. Even with a ten-week-old puppy, I would advise having an assistant for these exercises. Tie a length of stout string to one end of a meaty bone. Should the pup growl, have your assistant yank on the string to pull the bone away, and quickly cover it with a plastic garbage bucket. The plastic bucket may also be used to cover the pup's food bowl should the pup act up during food bowl exercises.

Don't waste time reprimanding the pup for growling. Instead, make sure to praise and reward your puppy as soon as she stops growling. Additionally, you must make sure that a growling puppy immediately loses her bone or food bowl. Many puppies will initially growl when food is removed. These are not bad dogs; they are normal dogs. Growling is quite natural. However, your puppy must learn that growling doesn't work so that this behavior does not escalate and continue into adolescence. As your puppy develops confidence, she will learn that there is no reason to growl because you have no intention of stealing her food. When the puppy stops growling, praise her, back away from the pup, and have her come, sit, and lie down. Give her back the object and then repeat the procedure.

A puppy may become protective and defensive if allowed to chew a bone in private and without interruption. Until you are quite comfortable taking bones away from your puppy, never let him have a bone on his own. Instead, say, "Off" and "Take it" as before, but hold on to the bone as your puppy chews. Periodically say, "Thank you!" and waggle a very tasty treat in front of the puppy's nose as you withdraw the bone. Hold the bone as the puppy eats the treats and then instruct the pup to sit and lie down before repeating the sequence over and over.

If you have problems with object and food guarding exercises, seek help immediately. Do not wait until your puppy is three months old.

THE FOOD BOWL

Many old-time dog-training books advise not going near a dog when she is eating. Whereas it may be sound advice to let a trust-worthy adult dog eat in peace, this does not mean letting un-trained puppies eat alone. If a pup grows up eating alone, she may not want her mealtimes disturbed as an adult. Eventually, someone is bound to bother the dog when she is eating, whereupon she may respond in a characteristically canine, food-protective fashion and growl, snarl, snap, lunge, and maybe bite.

By all means, tell people not to bother your dog when she is eating, but first be certain your puppy is totally trustworthy around her food bowl. Teach your puppy not simply to tolerate people around her food bowl, but to thoroughly look forward to dinner-time guests.

Hold your pup's bowl while she eats kibble. Offer tasty treats and handle the puppy, and she will learn her dinners are more enjoyable when people are present with petting and treats. Let the puppy eat kibble from her bowl, offer a tasty treat, and then temporarily remove the bowl as the puppy enjoys the treat. Then try removing the bowl prior to offering a treat. Your pup will soon look forward to your removing the bowl and the kibble, since it signals a tasty treat is imminent.

As your puppy is eating dry kibble from her bowl, quickly put your hand in the bowl and offer a tasty treat. Give your puppy time to reinvestigate the dry kibble, to check for more treats, and to recommence eating. Then plunge your hand in the bowl and offer another treat. Repeat the procedure several times. Your pup will soon become accustomed and look forward to sudden hand movements around her food bowl. This exercise impresses puppies to no end — it's like the magician who pulls a flower, an egg, or a dove from behind someone's ear.

Make sure your dogs sit for their supper.

Sit with your puppy while she is eating and have family members and friends walk by. Each time someone approaches, spoon a small dollop of canned food on top of the kibble. Your puppy will quickly make the association between approaching people and juicy canned food being added to her kibble. Later, have family and friends approach and toss a treat into the puppy's bowl. Soon your puppy will welcome the dinnertime presence and presents of people.

THE DELINQUENT WAITER ROUTINE

Have you ever been kept waiting for an hour in a restaurant, eating bread and drinking water, yet you haven't even ordered? "Where is that waiter? I wish he would hurry over." Well, the delinquent waiter routine prompts the same reaction in puppies. Most will beg you to approach their food bowl.

Weigh out your puppy's dinner kibble in one bowl on the counter and then put the pup's bowl on the floor with one piece of kibble. Try to capture your puppy's reaction on camera. She will look at the bowl with disbelief. Your pup will look back and forth between you and her bowl, gobble down the one piece of kibble, then thoroughly sniff the empty bowl. Casually walk away from the bowl and busy yourself. Maybe inquire as to whether or not your puppy enjoyed her dinner. "Was everything to your liking, Ma'am? Are you ready for the second course?" Wait until your puppy begs for more, walk over, pick up her bowl, place in one more piece of kibble, wait for the pup to sit, and then put her bowl on the floor.

Your puppy will become calmer and her manners will improve with each "course." Also, by feeding your puppy's dinner in many small courses, you will teach her to welcome your approaches.

PAPER TISSUE ISSUES

Years ago, I consulted on a case of a one-year-old dog who stole used Kleenex tissues and irritated his owner by playing Catch-Me-If-You-Can. The dog ran under a bed, the owner poked him with a broomstick, and the dog bit her on the wrist. I have since dealt with many similar cases. For paper-tissue theft to escalate to the point of both owner and dog physically abusing each other is extremely silly. If you don't want your dog to steal paper tissues, dispose of them. On the other hand, if the dog finds paper tissues intriguing, use them as lures and rewards in training, or give the dog one a day as a toy. It is essential that you teach your young puppy to exchange rolled newspaper, toilet rolls, or individual paper tissues for food treats so that he does not becomes possessive and protective of paper products.

"SHE'S A BIT TRICKY AROUND HER FOOD BOWL"

It is surprising how many adolescent dogs still display a tendency to guard food and objects, yet their owners do nothing about it. Whereas playful food- and object-guarding are quite normal, and to be expected in developing puppies, defensive guarding behavior cannot be allowed in adolescent or adult dogs. It is extremely easy to build your puppy's confidence so that she no longer feels the need to defend her food bowl, bones, and toys from people.

If you ever sense your puppy is even a little bit possessive or protective of any object, do something about it immediately. The requisite confidence-building exercises have all been described in this chapter. If you think the problem is beyond your control, seek help immediately while your puppy is still a puppy.

CHAPTER SEVEN

THE FIFTH DEVELOPMENTAL DEADLINE

Learning Bite Inhibition

(By Four and a Half Months of Age)

Puppies bite — and thank goodness they do. Puppy biting is a normal, natural, and necessary puppy behavior. Puppy play-biting is the means by which dogs develop bite inhibition and a soft mouth. The more your puppy bites and receives appropriate feedback, the safer his jaws will be in adulthood. It is the puppy that does not mouth and bite as a youngster whose adult bites are more likely to cause serious damage.

The puppy's penchant for biting results in numerous play-bites. Although its needle-sharp teeth make them painful, its weak jaws seldom cause serious harm. The developing puppy should learn that his bites can hurt long before he develops jaws strong enough to inflict injury. The greater the pup's opportunity to play-bite with people, other dogs, and other animals, the better his bite inhibition will be as an adult. For puppies that do not grow up with the benefit of regular interaction with other dogs and other animals, the responsibility of teaching bite inhibition lies entirely with the owner.

After diligently working on all the puppy socialization and handling exercises described in chapter 6, your dog will be unlikely to want to bite from fear or lack of confidence, because he likes people. However, should your dog snap or bite because he has been frightened or hurt, one hopes that he causes little if any damage, because he developed good bite inhibition during puppyhood. While it is difficult to socialize a dog and prepare it for every potentially scary eventuality, it is easy to ensure that as a puppy he develops reliable bite inhibition.

Even when provoked to bite, a dog with well-established bite inhibition seldom breaks the skin. As long as a dog's bite causes little or no damage, behavioral rehabilitation is comparatively easy and safe. But when your dog inflicts deep puncture wounds as an adult, rehabilitation is much more complicated, time-consuming, and potentially dangerous.

Good bite inhibition is the most important quality of any companion dog. Moreover, a dog must develop bite inhibition during puppyhood, before it is four and a half months old.

GOOD BITE INHIBITION

Good bite inhibition does not mean that your dog will never snap, lunge, nip, or bite. Good bite inhibition means that *should* the dog snap and lunge, his teeth will seldom make skin contact, and should the dog's teeth ever make skin contact, the inhibited "bite" will cause little, if any, damage.

CASE HISTORIES

No matter how well you try to socialize your dog and teach it to enjoy the company and actions of people, the unforeseen and unpredictable happens. Here are just a few case histories:

- A friend of the owner unintentionally slammed a car door on a dog's tail.

- A woman wearing high heels unintentionally stepped on her sleeping rottweiler's leg.

- An owner grabbed his Jack Russell by the collar.

- A groomer was combing out a wheaten's matted coat.

- A veterinarian was fixing a Bernese mountain dog's dislocated elbow.

- A visitor tripped and flew headlong to butt heads with an airedale terrier chewing his bone.

- A three-year-old child (who shall remain nameless) wearing a Superman cape jumped from a coffee table and landed on the ribcage of a sleeping malamute.

The rottweiler and Bernese both screamed. The Bernese lay perfectly still and did not attempt to bite. All the other dogs Grrrrwufffffed and quickly turned their muzzles towards the person. The malamute got up and left the room. Both the rottweiler and Jack Russell snapped and lunged, but neither made skin contact. The wheaten took hold of the groomer's arm and squeezed gently. The airedale nicked the visitor's cheek. All of these dogs were pretty friendly most of the time, but what is crucially important is that they had all developed stellar bite inhibition in puppyhood. Despite extreme fright or pain, bite inhibition instantly clicked in (within 0.04 of a second) to check the bite.

Consequently, none of these dogs caused any damage and all were successfully rehabilitated.

The dog with the trapped tail mutilated the person's arm with multiple deep bites. This dog was a breed most people consider to be extremely friendly and had been taken on numerous visits to schools and hospitals. Indeed, the dog was extremely friendly, but she had no bite inhibition. During puppyhood, she did not play with other dogs much, and her puppy biting behavior was infrequent and gentle. Because the dog had never displayed any signs of unfriendliness as an adult, there was no warning that she might bite. And because she had never snapped or bitten before, there was no warning that her bite would be serious. For a dog who is likely to spend a lot of time around people, being well-socialized but with poor bite inhibition is a dangerous combination.

Some people might feel that a dog is justified to bite in self-defense. But that is not what really happened in any of the above instances. In each case, the dog may have felt he was under attack, but in reality he bit a person who had no intention of hurting him. Whether you agree with this or not, the fact remains that we humans have been socialized not to attack our hairdressers, dentists, doctors, friends, and acquaintances when they unintentionally hurt us. Likewise, it is extremely easy, and essential, to train our dogs not to attack groomers, veterinarians, family, friends, and visitors.

THE BAD NEWS AND GOOD NEWS ABOUT DOG BITES

It is always upsetting when a dog growls, snaps, nips, or bites. But in the vast majority of bite cases, lack of injury provides reassuring proof that the dog has good bite inhibition. The dog may bite due to lack of socialization, but he does not do any damage because he has good bite inhibition.

It is reassuring for owners to know that if ever their dog were provoked and pushed to the limit, he would be strongly inhibited from hurting anyone. For example, if tormented by a child, the dog would only growl and snap and would not even make skin contact.

Customarily, dogs with good bite inhibition may be involved in numerous incidents before their snaps even touch the skin and certainly before their bites *break* the skin. Thus the owner has numerous warnings and ample time for rehabilitative socialization.

THE VERY GOOD, THE GOOD, THE BAD, AND THE UGLY

The very good: well-socialized with good bite inhibition

The very good is a wonderful dog who loves people and is highly unlikely to bite. Even if hurt or frightened, the dog is likely to yelp or move away. With extreme provocation, the dog might take hold, but it would be very unusual for the teeth to break the skin.

During puppyhood, the dog enjoyed many opportunities to play-fight with other puppies and dogs, and to mouth, play, and train with a wide variety of people.

Even though this is a wonderful dog, remember that socialization and bite inhibition training are lifelong endeavors. The dog may "bite" anyone but is unlikely to cause any harm.

The good: poorly socialized with good bite inhibition

The good is a dog who might snap, nip, or bite when provoked, but it is unlikely that the "bites" would break the skin. The dog is standoffish with strangers, prone to run away and hide, and only snaps, nips, or bites when pursued, crowded, or restrained.

The dog was raised with ample opportunity to mouth and play with other dogs and family members, but he did not get the opportunity to meet many other people during puppyhood.

The dog's scared and standoffish behavior provides repeated clear warning that the owner needs to rehabilitate the dog. Good bite inhibition enables the owner to socialize the dog safely. The dog's scared behavior provides ample warning for potential victims to stay away, and the dog's standoffish behavior normally keeps the dog away from strangers. Most likely victims are people who have to handle and examine the dog, such as veterinarians and groomers. This dog is likely to "bite" strangers, but is unlikely to cause much harm.

The bad: poorly socialized with bad bite inhibition

The bad is an apparent canine nightmare: a dog who doesn't like many people, barks and growls frequently, and is likely to lunge and bite and inflict deep punctures. Usually, initial incidents comprise a vocal lunge and a single deep bite, often with tearing as the dog pulls his head away in preparation for a hasty retreat.

Most likely the dog was raised in a backyard or kennel, or was confined indoors with limited contact with other dogs or people. Puppy play-biting was discouraged altogether.

The dog's saving grace is that he loudly and obviously advertises his lack of socialization, so that few people are silly enough to approach within biting distance. Consequently, incidents involving strangers are rare and involve extreme irresponsibility on the part of the owner, who has had numerous warnings to keep the dog away from people. In incidents with strangers, the dog usually makes a hasty retreat after a single bite. Usually, owners are the bite victims since only they are regularly close enough to the dog.

The ugly: well-socialized with bad bite inhibition

The ugly is the real canine nightmare — potentially an extremely dangerous dog! The dog's pleasant outward demeanor camouflages the real underlying problem — poor bite inhibition. This dog loves people and enjoys their company. He is unlikely to bite unless seriously provoked, or in extreme pain. However, should he bite, the punctures are deep and the damage is often extensive.

During puppyhood, this dog enjoyed many opportunities to play and train with a wide variety of people, but the owners probably discouraged mouthing and play-biting. Dog-dog socialization was insufficient and play-fighting was probably not allowed.

Anyone who enjoys socializing and playing with the dog may be bitten, including children, friends, family members, and strangers. Each incident may involve multiple bites since the dog is in no hurry to retreat.

Now before you worry that this sounds like your dog, please be objective. You do not necessarily have a dog with poor bite inhibition. What you have is a well-socialized dog with *unknown* bite inhibition. First, your dog is highly unlikely to bite. And if you continue socialization and handling exercises, he will be even less likely to bite. Second, should your dog bite someone, the odds are also very much in favor of your dog having good bite inhibition than not. However, you don't know for certain and so you should practice adult bite inhibition exercises (handfeeding, teeth cleaning, tug-o'-war, play-fighting) every day. A dog cannot have too soft a mouth.

Many people consider a dog a "good dog" until he growls or bites, whereupon he is branded a "bad dog." However, it's not really a case of "good" or "bad" dogs, but rather a case of "good" or "bad" socialization and bite inhibition training. A dog's level of socialization and whether or not he ever growls, snaps, nips, or bites depend on how well he was socialized in puppyhood. The degree of puppyhood socialization depends on the owner. But much more important than whether the dog growls and bites is whether the dog causes injury when he reacts defensively, that is, what level of bite inhibition he acquired in puppyhood, which also depends on the owner.

All owners should continue to socialize their dogs and practice handling, progressive desensitization, and bite inhibition exercises every day.

ACTUALLY, DOGS ARE LESS DEADLY THAN PEOPLE

Sadly, it is true that dogs occasionally mutilate and kill people. On average, each year in the United States dogs kill twenty people, half of them children. Such shocking events almost always make the front page, especially when the victim is a child. But even worse, in 2003 in the United States, more than two thousand children were killed by their parents. Moreover, these murders seldom make the national news. With over six children murdered by their parents each day, child murders are normally considered too commonplace to be newsworthy.

HUMAN BITE INHIBITION?

No dog is perfectly behaved, but luckily, most dogs are pretty well-socialized and have pretty good bite inhibition. Most dogs are basically friendly, even though they may occasionally be fearful and wary of some people some of the time. Also, although many dogs have growled, lunged, snapped, or even nipped someone at some time in their lives, very few dogs have ever inflicted any appreciable damage.

Perhaps a human analogy will help illustrate the crucial importance of bite inhibition. Few people can honestly say that they have never had a disagreement, never had an argument, or never laid a hand on someone in anger (especially when considering siblings, and, sadly, spouses and children). However, very few people have ever hurt another person so badly that they had to be admitted to the hospital. Thus, most people freely admit that they are sometimes disagreeable, argumentative, and occasionally physically aggressive. Even so, very few people have injured another person. Dogs are no different. Many dogs have several disagreements and arguments each day. Most dogs have been involved in full-contact fights at some time in their lives. But very, very few dogs have ever severely injured another dog or a person. This is the importance of bite inhibition.

BITE INHIBITION WITH OTHER DOGS

Dogfights offer a wonderful illustration of the effectiveness of solid bite inhibition. When dogs fight, it usually sounds like they are trying to kill each other, and it appears they forcibly bite each other over and over. However, when the dust settles and the dogs are examined, 99 percent of the time there are no puncture wounds whatsoever. Even though the fight was a frenzied flurry of gnashing jaws and both dogs were extremely worked up, no harm was done because both dogs had exquisitely fine-tuned bite inhibition, acquired during puppyhood. Puppies teach each other bite inhibition when play-fighting, their number one favorite activity.

Unless there are vaccinated adult dogs at home, your puppy must live within a temporary doggy social vacuum and dog-dog socialization must be postponed for a while. Until your puppy has acquired sufficient active immunity, it is too risky to allow it to socialize with dogs of dubious immunization history, or with dogs who may have stepped in the urine and feces of dogs potentially infected with parvovirus and other serious puppy diseases. However, as soon as your puppy has developed sufficient immunity to safely venture outdoors — at three months of age, at the earliest — catching up on dog-dog socialization is urgent. Enroll your puppy in puppy classes right away and take him for walks and to the local dog park several times a day. You will thank yourself for years to come. There is no greater enjoyment than being able to walk with your dog-friendly adult dog and watch him enjoy playing with other dogs.

Bite inhibition, however, cannot be put on hold. If there are no other dogs at home for your puppy to play with, *you* have to teach your puppy bite inhibition until he is old enough to go to puppy classes.

Young puppies have frequent and lengthy fights. Most fights are an essential ingredient of normal puppy play, but puppies also have occasional scraps to establish and maintain rank. Frequent play-fighting and occasional rank disputes are essential to fine-tune bite inhibition.

BITE INHIBITION WITH PEOPLE

Even if your puppy has a couple of canine buddies at home, you will still need to teach your puppy to inhibit the force and frequency of her bites toward people. Additionally, you must teach your puppy how to react when frightened or hurt by people. She should by all means yelp, but she should not bite and she should never bear down.

Even if your dog is friendly and mouths gently, by five months of age at the very latest, she must be taught never to touch any person's body or clothing with her jaws unless requested. Whereas mouthing is essential for puppies and acceptable from a young adolescent dog, it would be utterly inappropriate for an older adolescent or adult dog to mouth visitors and strangers. It would be absolutely unacceptable for a six-month-old dog to approach a child and take hold of her arm, no matter how gentle, friendly, and playful the dog's intentions. It would frighten the living daylights out of the child, to say nothing of her parents.

BITE INHIBITION EXERCISES

Please read this section extremely carefully. I shall repeat over and over: teaching bite inhibition is the most important part of your puppy's entire education.

Certainly puppy biting behavior must eventually be eliminated. We cannot have an adult dog playfully mauling family, friends, and strangers in the manner of a young puppy. However, it is essential that this be done gradually and progressively via a systematic two-step process: first, to inhibit the force of puppy bites, and, second, to lessen the frequency of puppy bites.

Ideally, the two phases should be taught in sequence, but with more active puppy biters you may wish to work on both stages at the same time. In either case, you must teach your puppy to bite or mouth gently before puppy biting behavior is eliminated altogether.

INHIBITING THE FORCE OF BITES

The first step is to stop your puppy from hurting people: to teach him to inhibit the force of his play-bites. It is not necessary to reprimand the pup, and certainly physical punishments are not called for. But it is essential to let your puppy know that bites can hurt. A simple "Ouch!" is usually sufficient. When the puppy backs off, take a short time-out to "lick your wounds," instruct your pup to come, sit, and lie down to apologize and make up. Then resume playing. If your puppy does not respond to your yelp by easing up or backing off, an effective technique is to call the puppy a "Bully!" and then leave the room and shut the door. Allow the pup a minute or two time-out to reflect on the association between his painful bite and the immediate departure of his favorite human chewtoy. Then return to make up. It is important to show that you still love your puppy, only that his painful bites are objectionable. Have your pup come and sit and then resume playing once more.

It is much better for you to walk away from the pup than to physically restrain him or remove him to his confinement area at a time when he is biting too hard. So make a habit of playing with your puppy in his long-term confinement area. This technique is remarkably effective with lead-headed dogs, since it is precisely the way puppies learn to inhibit the force of their bites when playing with each other. If one puppy bites another too hard, the bitee yelps and playing is postponed while he licks his wounds. The biter soon learns that hard bites interrupt an otherwise enjoyable play session. He learns to bite more softly once play resumes.

The more a puppy bites you and receives appropriate feedback, the better his bite inhibition and the more reliable his jaws in adulthood. Appropriate feedback to reduce the force of puppy bites comprises praising the puppy for gentle mouthing, yelping and having a brief pause from play when the pressure increases, and yelping and having a thirty-second time-out from play following painful bites. After each pause or time-out, remember to instruct your puppy to come, sit, and lie down before resuming play.

The next step is to eliminate bite pressure entirely, even though the "bites" no longer hurt. While your puppy is chewing his human chewtoy, wait for a bite that is harder than the rest and respond as if it really hurt, even though it didn't: "Ouch, you worm! Gennntly! That really hurt me, you bully!" Your puppy begins to think, "Good heavens! These humans are soooooo sensitive. I'll have to be really careful when mouthing their delicate skin." And that's precisely what you want your pup to think: that he needs to be extremely careful and gentle when playing with people.

Your pup should learn not to hurt people well before he is three months old. Ideally, by the time he is four and a half months old — before he develops strong jaws and adult canine teeth — he should no longer be exerting any pressure when mouthing.

DECREASING THE FREQUENCY OF MOUTHING

Once your puppy has been taught to mouth gently, it is time to reduce the frequency of mouthing. Your pup must learn that mouthing is okay, but she must stop when requested. Why? Because it is inconvenient to drink a cup of tea or to answer the telephone with fifty pounds of wriggling pup dangling from your wrist. That's why.

It is better to first teach "Off" using food as both a distraction and a reward. The deal is this: once I say, "Off," if you don't touch the food treat in my hand for just one second, I'll say, "Take it" and you can have it. Once your pup has mastered this simple task, up the ante to two or three seconds of noncontact, and then to five, eight, twelve, twenty, and so on. Count out the seconds and praise the dog with each second: "Good Dog One, Good Dog Two, Good Dog Three," and so forth. If the pup touches the treat before you are ready to give it, simply start the count from zero again. Your pup quickly learns that once you say, "Off," she cannot have the treat until she has not touched it, for say eight seconds, so the quickest way to get the treat is not to touch it for the first eight seconds. In addition, regular hand-feeding during this exercise encourages your pup's soft mouth.

Once your pup understands the "Off" request, use food as a lure and a reward to teach her to let go when mouthing. Say, "Off," and waggle some food as a lure to entice your pup to let go and sit. Then praise the pup and give the food as a reward when she does so.

The main point of this exercise is to practice stopping the pup from mouthing, and so each time your puppy obediently ceases and desists, resume playing once more. Stop and start the session many times over. Also, since the puppy wants to mouth, the best reward for stopping mouthing is to allow her to mouth again. When you decide to stop the mouthing session altogether, say, "Off," and then offer your puppy a Kong stuffed with kibble.

If ever your pup refuses to release your hand when requested, say "Bully!" rapidly extricate your hand from her mouth, and storm out of the room mumbling, "Right. That's done it! You've ruined it! Finished! Over! No more!" and shut the door in her face. Give the pup a couple of minutes on her own and then go back to call her to come and sit and make up before continuing the mouthing game.

By the time your pup is five months old she must have a mouth as soft as a fourteen-year-old working Labrador retriever: your puppy should never initiate mouthing unless requested, she should never exert any pressure when mouthing, and she should stop mouthing and calm down immediately upon request by any family member.

Whether or not you allow your adult dog to mouth on request is up to you. For most owners, I recommend that they teach their dog to discontinue mouthing people altogether by the time he is six to eight months old. However, it is essential to continue bite inhibition exercises. Otherwise, your dog's bite will begin to drift and become harder as he grows older. It is important to regularly handfeed your dog and clean his teeth each day, since these exercises involve a human hand in his mouth.

For owners who have good control over their dog, there is no better way to maintain the dog's soft mouth than by regular play-fighting. However, to prevent your puppy from getting out of control and to fully realize the many benefits of play-fighting, you must play by the rules and teach your dog to play by the rules. Play-fighting rules are described in detail in the *Preventing Aggression* behavior booklet.

Play-fighting teaches your puppy to mouth only hands, which are extremely sensitive to pressure, but never clothing. Shoelaces, ties, trousers, and hair have no nerves and cannot feel. Therefore you cannot provide the necessary feedback when your pup begins to mouth too hard and too close to your skin. The play-fighting game also teaches your dog that he must adhere to rules regarding his jaws, regardless of how worked up he may be. Basically, play-fighting gives you the opportunity to practice controlling your puppy when he is excited. It is important to establish such control in a structured setting before real-life situations occur.

Establishing bite inhibition is so vitally important that a good 90 percent of puppy play involves biting each other. Perhaps we should learn from our dogs.

OUT-OF-CONTROL PLAY SESSIONS

Some owners, especially adult males, adolescent males, and boys, quickly let play-mouthing sessions get out of control. This is why many dog-training texts recommend not indulging in games such as play-fighting or tug-of-war. The whole point about playing these games is to improve your control. And if you play these games by the rules, you will soon have excellent control over your puppy's mouthing behavior, vocal output, energy level, and activity. However, if you do not play by the rules, you will soon have an adult dog who is dangerously out of control.

I have a simple rule with my dogs: no one is allowed to interact or play with them unless they have demonstrated that they can get them to come, sit, lie down, speak, and shush. This rule applies to everyone, especially family, friends, and visitors — that is, the people most likely to ruin your dog's behavior. For active games, such as tug-o'-war, play-fighting, and a unique version of football, I have an additional rule: No one may play with the dogs unless at any time they can immediately get the dog to stop playing and sit or lie down.

Practice "Off," "Sit," and "Settle Down" many times during your puppy's play sessions, and you will soon have an easily controllable adult dog, one that has learned to listen to you no matter how excited and worked up he may be. Do not play with your pup without frequent interruptions. Have short time-outs at least every fifteen seconds or so to check that you're in control and can easily and quickly get the puppy to let go, calm down, and settle down. The more you practice, the more control you'll have.

A BIG MISTAKE

A common mistake is to punish the pup in an attempt to get him to stop biting. At best, the puppy no longer bites those family members who can effectively punish him but instead directs his biting toward those who have no control — for example, children. What is worse, because the pup does not mouth them, parents are often unaware of the child's plight. Worse still, the puppy may no longer mouth people at all. Hence, he receives no training for inhibiting the force of his bites. All is fine until someone accidentally treads on the dog's foot, or shuts the car door on his tail, whereupon the dog bites and the bite punctures the skin because there has been insufficient bite inhibition training.

PUPPIES WITH SOFT MOUTHS

Many gundog breeds, especially Spaniels (and especially the nice Spaniels), have extremely soft mouths as puppies and therefore receive limited feedback that their jaws can hurt. If a puppy does not frequently mouth, bite, and does not occasionally bite hard, this is serious. The puppy must learn his limits, and he can only learn his limits by exceeding them during development and receiving the appropriate feedback. Again, the solution lies with puppy classes and off-leash play sessions with other puppies.

PUPPIES THAT DON'T BITE

Shy dogs seldom socialize or play with other dogs or strangers. Hence they do not play-bite, nor do they learn to reduce the force of their bites. The classic case history describes a dog who didn't mouth or bite much as a pup and never bit anyone as an adult — until an unfamiliar child tripped and fell on the dog while it was gnawing on a bone. Not only did the dog bite, but his first bite left deep puncture wounds because he had developed no bite inhibition. With shy puppies, socialization is of paramount importance and time is of the essence.

Similarly, some Asian breeds have an extremely high degree of fidelity toward their owners, and, consequently, tend to be fairly standoffish with other dogs or human strangers. Some restrict their mouthing and biting to members of the family, and some simply do not mouth at all. Hence, they never learn to inhibit the force of their jaws.

Nonbiting puppies must be socialized immediately. They must commence play-fighting and play-biting well before they are three months old. Socialization and initiating play are best accomplished by promptly signing up for puppy classes.

SPEED OF DEVELOPMENT

The large working dog breeds develop slowly and, as long as they have not developed problems, may delay starting puppy classes until they are four months old. (They should start by four and a half months at the latest.) Smaller breeds, however, especially cattle dogs, develop much faster, and waiting until they are four months old is too late. Cattle dogs, working sheep dogs, toys, and terriers need to be enrolled in puppy classes as soon as is safe, and certainly by three and a half months of age at the latest.

Of course, regardless of the size and speed of development of your puppy, to get the most out of his formal education, enroll in a class when your puppy is three months old and then enroll in a second class when he is four and a half months old.

PUPPY SCHOOL

As soon as your puppy is three months old, there is an urgent need to play catch-up in terms of socialization and confidence-building with other dogs. At the very latest, before he is eighteen weeks old, your pup should start puppy training classes.

Four and a half months marks a critical juncture in your dog's development, the point at which he changes from puppy to adolescent, sometimes virtually overnight. You certainly want to be enrolled in class before your pup collides with adolescence. I cannot overemphasize the importance of placing yourself under the guidance and tutelage of a professional pet dog trainer during your dog's difficult transition from puppyhood to adolescence.

Puppy classes allow your pup to develop canine social savvy while playing with other puppies in a nonthreatening and controlled setting. Shy and fearful pups quickly gain confidence in leaps and bounds and bullies learn to tone it down and be gentle.

Puppy play sessions are crucially important. Play is essential for pups to build confidence and learn canine social etiquette, so that later on as socialized adult dogs they prefer playing to either fighting or taking flight. If not sufficiently socialized as puppies, dogs generally lack the confidence to have fun and play as adults. Moreover, once they are fearful or aggressive as adults, dogs can be difficult to rehabilitate. Luckily, these potentially serious problems with adult dogs are easily prevented in puppyhood, simply by letting puppies play with each other. So give your puppy this opportunity. It's not fair to condemn your dog to a lifetime of social worry and anxiety by denying him the opportunity to play during puppyhood.

This is not to say that a socialized dog will never spook or scrap. A socialized dog may be momentarily startled, but he gets over it quickly. Unsocialized dogs do not. Also, socialized dogs, which have encountered all sizes and sorts of dogs, are better equipped to deal with occasional encounters with unsocialized or unfriendly dogs.

DOG-DOG VS. DOG-PEOPLE SOCIALIZATION

Training a dog to be people-friendly and especially to enjoy the company of its immediate human family is the second most important item in your puppy's education — much more important than socializing him to other dogs. (As we all know by now, the most important item in your puppy's educational curriculum is, of course, bite inhibition.)

Although a few common sense precautions make it possible to live quite happily with a dog who does not get along with other dogs, it can be extremely difficult and even dangerous to live with a dog who does not like people — especially if it doesn't like family members! So people-friendliness is a much more important doggy quality than dog-friendliness.

But it is truly wonderful when a dog is dog-friendly, having had ample opportunity to meet and play with other dogs on walks and in dog parks. Unfortunately, few suburban dogs are regularly walked or even given the opportunity to interact with other dogs. For many dog owners, dog-friendliness is simply not a top priority. On the other hand, for owners who consider dog-friendliness important, in fact a major reason for having a dog, their dogs are presumably walked and/or taken to dog parks regularly and so are likely to grow up to be sociable with other dogs. Even so, people-friendliness is still much more important than dog-friendliness, because every day when walked they are likely to meet many strangers, often children.

Most puppy classes are family-oriented, so your pup will have opportunities to socialize with all sorts of people — men, women, and especially children. And then there is the training game. It will blow your mind how much your pup learns in just her very first lesson. Dogs learn to come, sit, and lie down when requested, to stand still and roll over for examination, to listen to their owners, and to ignore distractions. Additionally, of course, puppy classes are an absolute blast! You will never forget your pup's first night in class. Puppy classes are an adventure, both for you and for your dog.

Remember, you are attending puppy class for *you* to learn! And there's still an awful lot to learn. You'll pick up numerous useful tips for resolving behavior problems. You'll learn how to control the rambunctiousness that is inevitably part of doggy adolescence. But, most important of all, you'll learn how to control your puppy's biting behavior.

THE ULTIMATE REASON FOR PUPPY CLASS

The number one reason for attending puppy class is to provide your puppy with the very best opportunity to fine-tune its bite inhibition. Whether your puppy is still biting you too much and harder than you would like, or whether she is biting less than necessary to develop reliable bite inhibition, puppy play sessions are the solution. Other puppies are the very best teachers. They say, "Bite me too hard and I'm not going to play with you anymore!" Since puppies want to spend all their time play-fighting and play-biting, they end up teaching other puppies bite inhibition.

Classes of young puppies of about the same age generate high energy and activity levels, pretty much on par with groups of children of similar ages. Each puppy stimulates the others to give chase and play-fight, such that the frequency of bites during puppy play is astronomical. Moreover, each puppy tends to rev up all the others, such that the physical nature of the play and the force of play-bites progressively increase to the point where one puppy predictably bites another too hard and receives the appropriate feedback. A young puppy's skin is extremely sensitive, so pups are likely to provide immediate and convincing feedback when bitten too hard. In fact, a pup is likely to receive better feedback regarding the force of his bites during a single one-hour puppy class than he would all week from his owner at home. Moreover, much of the pup's bite inhibition with other dogs will generalize to good bite inhibition with people, making the pup easier to train and control at home.

Now, as mentioned earlier, even well-socialized dogs may have occasional disagreements and squabbles. After all, who doesn't? But

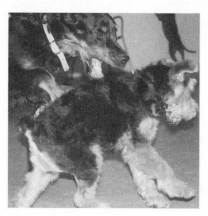 

Other puppies are the best teachers of bite inhibition. By four months of age, puppy play is almost entirely comprised of chasing and biting each other. Do remember, though, to frequently check that your puppy is not out of control. Interrupt your puppy's play every fifteen seconds by taking hold of his collar, calming him down, and maybe instructing him to sit before allowing him to resume play. Remember, you want your puppy to grow up to be sociable and controllable. You do not want your puppy to become an uncontrollable, hyperactive social loon.

just as we have learned how to resolve disagreements with each other and with our dogs in a socially acceptable manner without tearing flesh or breaking bones, so can socialized dogs. Although it is unrealistic to expect dogs never to squabble and scrap, it is absolutely realistic to expect dogs to settle their differences without mutilating people or other dogs. It all depends on the level of bite inhibition they develop while mouthing other puppies in play. So get your puppy enrolled in puppy class right away. Have him develop a supersoft mouth so that all his woofs are friendly and furry.

THE VET SAYS OUR PUPPY IS TOO YOUNG FOR CLASS

Understandably, veterinarians care about the physical health of their patients. Common and serious infectious diseases such as parvovirus and distemper are a big concern with young puppies, who require a series of immunizations to produce solid immunity. By three months of age, puppies only have 70–75 percent immunity, so there is justifiable concern that they are still at risk if exposed to infection. But puppy classrooms are pretty safe places, since only vaccinated puppies are present and the floors are regularly cleaned and sterilized. Besides, your puppy's physical health is only part of the picture. Psychological and behavioral health are equally important.

A puppy's risk of infection depends on his level of immunity and the infectiousness of the environment. A puppy's immunity increases with successive immunizations until it approaches 99 percent immunity at five months of age. Different environments range from relatively safe to extremely hazardous. But no animal is 100 percent immune to disease, and no environment is 100 percent safe.

If physical health were the only concern, I would advise that puppies not venture out into potentially infected areas until they are at least five to six months old. However, a puppy's behavior, temperament, bite inhibition, and mental well-being are equally as important as physical health. Each year in the United States, an average of five puppies per veterinary clinic die from parvovirus, whereas several hundred are euthanized because of behavior and temperament problems. Indeed, behavior problems are dogs' most common terminal illness during their first year of life. And just as a developing puppy needs immunizations against infectious diseases, he also requires social and educational "immunizations" to prevent him from developing behavior and temperament problems. For all-around health, a young puppy must receive immunization against disease, but he must also get out and about on walks, to dog parks, and to puppy classes as soon as possible.

The older the puppy, the better his immunity. Keep your young puppy as safe as possible — at home — but as he gets older he may venture out to less safe areas, such as puppy classes. Once your adolescent dog has maximal immunity, he may more safely frequent hazardous areas such as sidewalks, dog parks, veterinary waiting rooms, and veterinary parking lots.

CARRY YOUR PUPPY

Perhaps even more than sidewalks and dog parks, the waiting room floor and parking lot of the veterinary clinic are the two most hazardous areas for puppies with incomplete immunity. While examination tables are washed and sterilized after every patient, waiting room floors are generally disinfected only once a day and parking lots hardly ever. Dogs urinate and defecate in the parking lot and occasionally in the waiting room. Urine may be contaminated with leptospirosis or distemper virus, and feces may be contaminated with parvovirus, coronavirus, or a variety of internal parasites. When in the waiting room, keep your puppy on your lap at all times. Alternatively, leave your puppy in the car and carry him directly to the examination room table when your turn comes.

It is a sad fact of life that your puppy is always at risk. For example, dried feces carrying parvovirus may blow in the wind and end up in your garden or home. Or a family member could step in infected urine and feces and track it through the home. So maintain routine hygiene and leave outdoor shoes outside. The safest place for your young puppy is inside your home or fenced backyard. Keep him there until he is three months old. Before your puppy is three months old, he has household manners to master and many pressing socialization exercises to do in the safety of your home. Other relatively safe places include your car and the homes and fenced yards of family and friends. So it is possible for your pup to begin to safely explore the world at large. Just remember to carry him between house and car.

As I've said, indoor puppy classes provide a pretty safe environment, but I would still recommend carrying the pup between car and class. Luckily, the breeds that sometimes have immunity problems — Rotties and Dobies, for example — are slow developers, and it is fine to delay starting class until they are four months old. I actually prefer bigger, slower-maturing dogs to start class at four months so that adolescent problems can be dealt with while the dog is still in class. Otherwise, if a big dog starts class at three months of age, he will graduate at four and a half months and the owner is still under the misapprehension that they are living with a teddy bear.

I would similarly advise to delay taking your puppy to dog parks or for walks in public places frequented by other dogs until he is at least four months old. You can always practice leash-walking around your house and yard before performing in public, and you should be inviting people to your house on a regular basis.

BUT OUR PUPPY'S GREAT WITH OUR OTHER DOG AT HOME

Your puppy may be Mr. Sociable with your other dog, but you're in for a shock when your puppy goes out alone, whether for a walk on the street, to a dog park, or to training class. You will quickly find that your dog is not socialized at all. Instead, he will likely run and hide and defensively growl, lunge, and snap. Your puppy may appear to be extremely well-socialized and friendly at home, but he is only socialized and friendly to one dog. Also, he has likely become overdependent on one dog, and when he goes out alone for the first time, he will fall apart, missing the security and company of his best friend and bodyguard, your other dog.

It is wonderful that your puppy gets along with your other dogs at home. However, to learn how to get along with unfamiliar dogs, your puppy needs to meet unfamiliar dogs at puppy class, on walks, and in dog parks.

Using a Kong to lure/reward train a pup to sit at Manhattan Dog Training in New York City.

Socialization requires meeting a variety of dogs. To keep a socialized puppy socialized, he needs to meet unfamiliar dogs every day. So walk your puppy and take him on regular trips to dog parks. And be sure to enroll him in puppy classes.

Puppies being trained to periodically sit and calm down during the play session in Sirius® Puppy Training classes at Citizen Canine in Oakland, California.

LOOKING FOR A PUPPY CLASS

Here are a few tips: avoid puppy classes that advocate the use of any metal collar or any means of physical punishment that frightens, harms, or causes pain to your pup. Push-pull, leash-jerk, grab-and-shake, alpha rollover, and domination techniques are now considered ineffective, besides being adversarial and unpleasant. These out-of-date methods are now, thank goodness, by and large a thing of the past.

Remember, this is your puppy. Her education, safety, and sanity are in your hands. There are so many good puppy schools. Search until you find one.

Look for puppy classes where the pups are given ample opportunity to play together off-leash and where pups are frequently — at least every fifteen seconds — trained and settled down during the play session, using toys and treats and fun and games. Off-leash puppy play is vital, but equally as important, the play session must include many short training interludes so owners may practice controlling their pup when he is worked up and distracted. Look for classes where puppies learn quickly and owners are pleased with their puppies' progress. And above all look for classes where the puppies are having a good time!

You be the judge, and judge wisely. Choosing a suitable puppy class is one of your most important puppy husbandry decisions.

To receive a list of Certified Pet Dog Trainers in your area contact the Association of Pet Dog Trainers. Check online at www.apdt.com or call 1-800-PET-DOGS.

CHAPTER EIGHT

THE SIXTH DEVELOPMENTAL DEADLINE

The World at Large

(By Five Months and Thereafter)

B y now you're probably quite exhausted by your puppy raising efforts. Hopefully, though, you are justifiably proud of
your well-mannered, well-behaved, highly socialized dog
with dependable bite inhibition. The challenge now is to maintain
your dog's stellar qualities.

The prime purpose of puppy husbandry is to produce a
friendly, confident, and biddable pup, so that you can face the
behavior and training challenges of your dog's adolescence, and
your dog can deal with the immense social upheaval that dogs,

especially males, face as they navi-
gate adolescence. It is much easier
to approach doggy adolescence
with an already socialized and
well-trained dog. However, maintaining your dog's socialization
and training through his adolescence can be tricky if you don't
know what to expect and how to
deal with it.

CHANGES TO EXPECT AS YOUR DOG NAVIGATES ADOLESCENCE

Behavior is always changing, sometimes for the better, sometimes for the worse. Things will continue to improve if you continue working with your adolescent dog, but they will definitely get worse if you don't. Both behavior and temperament will tend to stabilize, for better or worse, as your dog matures around his second birthday for small dogs or third birthday for large dogs. But until then, if you don't keep on top of things, there can be precipitous and catastrophic changes in your dog's temperament and manners. Even when your dog reaches maturity, you should always be on the alert for the emergence of unwanted behaviors or traits, which you must quickly nip in the bud before they become hard-to-break habits.

A dog's adolescence is the time when everything starts to fall apart, unless you make a concerted effort to see it through to the stability of adulthood. Your dog's adolescence is a critical time. Ignore your dog's education now and you will soon find yourself living with an ill-mannered, undersocialized, hyperactive animal. Here are some things to watch for:

Household etiquette may deteriorate over time, especially if you start taking your dog's housetraining and other good behavior for granted. But if you taught your pup well in his earlier months, the drift in household etiquette will be slow until your dog reaches his sunset years, when housetraining especially tends to suffer.

Basic manners may take a sharp dive when puppy collides with adolescence. Lure/reward training your puppy was easy: you taught your pup to eagerly come, follow, sit, lie down, stand still, roll over, and look up to you with unwavering attention and respect because you were your pup's sun, moon, and stars. But now your dog is developing adult doggy interests, such as investigating other dogs' rear ends, sniffing urine and feces on the grass, rolling in unidentifiable smelly stuff, and chasing squirrels. Your dog's interests may quickly become distractions to training, so that your dog will continue sniffing another dog's rear end rather than come running when called. (What a scary thought, that your dog would prefer another dog's rear end to you!) All of a sudden he won't come, won't sit, won't settle down and stay, but instead jumps up, pulls on-leash, and becomes hyperactive.

Bite inhibition tends to drift as your dog gets older and develops more powerful jaws. Giving your dog ample opportunity to wrestle with other dogs, regularly handfeeding kibble and treats, and periodically examining and cleaning your dog's teeth are the best exercises to ensure that your adolescent dog maintains his soft mouth.

Socialization often heads downhill during adolescence, sometimes surprisingly precipitously. As they get older, dogs have fewer opportunities to meet unfamiliar people and dogs. Puppy classes and parties are often a thing of the past and most owners have established a set routine by the time their dog is five or six months old. At home, the dog interacts with the same familiar friends and family, and is walked, if at all, on the same route to the same dog park, where he encounters the same people and the same dogs. Consequently, many adolescent dogs become progressively desocialized toward unfamiliar people and dogs until eventually they become intolerant of all but a small inner circle of friends.

If your adolescent dog does not get out and about regularly and few unfamiliar people come to the house, his desocialization may be alarmingly rapid. At five months your dog was a social butterfly with nothing but wiggles and wags when greeting people, but by eight months of age he has become defensive and lacking in confidence: he barks and backs off, or he snaps and lunges with hackles raised. A previously friendly adolescent dog might suddenly and without much warning be spooked by a household guest.

Puppy socialization was a prelude to your safe and enjoyable continued socialization of your adolescent dog. However, your adolescent dog must continue meeting unfamiliar people regularly.

Similarly, successful adolescent socialization makes it possible for you to safely and enjoyably continue to socialize your adult dog. Socialization is an ongoing process.

Dog-dog socialization also deteriorates during adolescence, often at an alarming rate, especially for very small and very large dogs. First, teaching a dog to get along with every other dog is difficult. Groups of wild canids — wolves, coyotes, jackals — seldom welcome strangers into their midst, but that's exactly what we expect of *Canis familiaris*. Second, it is unrealistic to expect a dog to be best friends with every dog. Much like people, dogs have special friends, casual acquaintances, and individuals they don't particularly like. Third, it is quite natural for dogs, especially males, to squabble. In fact, it is a rare male dog who has never been involved in some physical altercation. Everything was fine with young pups playing in class and in parks, but with adolescent dogs, the scraps, the arguments, and even the play-fighting seem all too real.

The very best way to keep your socialized puppy socialized is by regular walks and visits to your local dog parks.

A dog's first adolescent fight often marks the beginning of the end of his socialization with other dogs. Again, this is especially true for very small and very large dogs. Owners of small dogs are understandably concerned about their dog's safety and may be disinclined to allow their dogs to run with the big dogs. Here is where socialization starts downhill and the small dog becomes increasingly snappy and scrappy. Similarly, owners of large dogs (especially the working breeds) are understandably concerned that their dogs might hurt smaller dogs. Here too, socialization goes downhill and the big dog becomes increasingly snappy and scrappy. Now we're in a vicious circle: the less the dog is socialized, the more likely he is to fight and thus be less socialized.

The first couple of visits to a dog park can be a little scary for your dog. It is okay for your puppy to hide or seek your reassurance. Immediately pick up your puppy if you are at all concerned for her safety. Otherwise, try your best not to unintentionally reinforce needy behavior by soothing or petting your puppy while she is hiding. Instead, try to let other people and dogs coax your pup into the open, and then praise your dog enthusiastically whenever she leaves her hiding place.

"HE FIGHTS ALL THE TIME!
HE'S TRYING TO KILL OTHER DOGS!"

The fury and noise of a dogfight can be quite scary for onlookers, especially the dogs' owners. In fact, nothing upsets owners more than a dogfight. Consequently, owners must strive to be objective when assessing the seriousness of a dogfight. Otherwise, a single dogfight can put an end to their dogs' socialization. In most cases, a dogfight is highly stereotyped, controlled, and relatively safe. With appropriate feedback from the owner, the prognosis for resolution is good. On the other hand, irrational or emotional feedback, besides being upsetting for the owner, can exacerbate the problem for the dog.

It is extremely common for dogs, especially adolescent males, to posture, stare, growl, snarl, snap, and maybe fight. This is not "bad" dog behavior, but rather reflects what dogs normally do. Dogs do not write letters of complaint or call their lawyers. Growling and fighting, however, almost always reflect an underlying lack of confidence, characteristic of male adolescence. Given time and continued socialization, adolescent dogs normally develop confidence and no longer feel the need to continually prove themselves. To have the confidence to continue socializing a dog who has instigated a fight, the owner must convince himself that his "fighting dog" is not dangerous. A dog may be obnoxious and a royal pain, but this does not mean he would hurt another dog. Whereas growling and fighting are normal developmental behaviors, causing harm to other dogs is not.

First, you need to ascertain the severity of the problem. Second, you need to make sure you react appropriately when your dog fights, and give appropriate feedback when he doesn't.

To know whether or not you have a problem, establish your dog's Fight-Bite Ratio. To do this you need to answer two questions: How many times has your dog been involved in a fight? And in how many fights did the other dog have to be taken to the veterinarian?

Ten-to-Zero is a common Fight-Bite Ratio for a one- to two-year-old male dog, that is, ten full-contact fights with opponents taking zero trips to the vet. We do not have a serious problem here. Obviously the dog is not trying to kill the other dog, since he hasn't caused any injury in ten fights. The dog would have caused damage if he had meant to. Moreover, on each occasion, the dog adhered to the Marquis of Dogsberry Fighting Rules by restricting bites to the other dog's scruff, neck, head, and muzzle. Surely, there is no better proof of the effectiveness of bite inhibition than, when in a fighting frenzy, one dog grasps another by the soft part of its throat and yet no damage is done.

This is not a dangerous dog. It is merely obnoxious in the inimitable manner of male adolescents. Yes, the dog is a bit of a pain, but he has wonderful bite inhibition (established during puppyhood) and has never injured another dog. Solid evidence of reliable bite inhibition — ten fights with zero bites while adhering to fighting rules — makes it extremely unlikely that this dog will ever harm another dog.

Fights are bad news, but they usually provide good news! As long as your dog never harms another dog, each fight provides impressive additional proof that your dog has reliable bite inhibition. Your dog may lack confidence and social grace, but at least his jaws are safe. He is not a dangerous dog. Consequently, resolution of the problem will be fairly simple. Of course, you still have an obnoxious dog in dire need of retraining, since your dog is annoying other dogs and owners just as much as he annoys you. Call the Association of Pet Dog Trainers at 1-800-PET-DOGS to find a local Difficult Dog or Growl class.

On the other hand, if your dog has inflicted serious wounds to the limbs and abdomen of his opponents in a number of his fights, then you have a serious problem. This is a dangerous dog, since he has no bite inhibition. Obviously, the dog should be muzzled whenever on public property. The prognosis is poor, treatment will be complicated, time-consuming, potentially dangerous, requiring expert help, and certainly with no guarantee of a positive outcome. No dog problem presents such a marked contrast between prevention and treatment.

Canine social greetings normally involve a thorough investigation of each other's private parts. Reading a dog's olfactory "business card" is usually a prelude to play. Praise your puppy every time he greets another dog. Do not take your puppy's friendly greetings for granted; his first squabble is probably only months, or weeks, away. If you don't want your dog to get into scraps, you must let him know how pleased you are when he greets other dogs and plays in a friendly fashion.

An adult fighter with no bite inhibition is the very hardest dog to rehabilitate, but prevention in puppyhood is easy, effortless, and enjoyable: simply enroll your puppy in puppy classes and take him to the park regularly. Do not wait for your adolescent dog to get into a fight to let him know you don't like it. Instead, make a habit of praising and rewarding your puppy every time he greets another dog in a friendly fashion. I know it may sound a little silly — praising your harmless, wiggly four-month-old male pup and offering a food treat every time he doesn't fight — but it's the best way to prevent fighting from becoming a serious problem.

THE SECRET TO ADOLESCENT SUCCESS

Always make a point of praising your dog and offering a couple of treats whenever he eliminates in the right place. Keep a treat container by your dog's toilet area. You need to be there anyway to inspect and pick up your dog's feces before the stool becomes home and dinner for several hundred baby flies. Remember, you want your dog to want to eliminate in his toilet area and to be highly motivated to do so, even when he develops geriatric incontinence.

Similarly, a stuffed Kong a day will continue to keep the behavior doctor away. Your dog still needs some form of occupational therapy to idle away the time when left at home alone. Nothing will prevent household problems, such as destructive chewing, excessive barking, and hyperactivity, or alleviate boredom, stress, and anxiety as effectively as stuffing your dog's daily diet of kibble into a few Kongs.

For your adolescent dog to continue to be reliably obedient and willingly compliant, you must integrate short training interludes, especially emergency sits and long settle-downs, into walks, play sessions, and your dog's other enjoyable day-to-day activities. Maintaining your dog's manners through adolescence is easy if you know how to, but extremely difficult if you don't. See the sections "Training on Walks" on page 176 and "Integrate Training and Lifestyle" on page 189.

Should socialization ever fail and your dog snap, lunge, or nip, you will be thankful that you had the good sense to take your puppy to classes where she learned reliable bite inhibition. Your dog's defensive actions cause no harm but they warn you that you'd better quickly revamp your dog's socialization program and maintain her bite inhibition exercises before it happens again, which it will. Continue bite inhibition exercises indefinitely. Occasionally handfeed your dog and examine her muzzle and teeth (and maybe clean them) on a regular basis.

The secret to a well-socialized adult dog is at least one walk a day and a couple of trips a week to the dog park. Try to find different walks and different dog parks, so that your dog meets a variety of dogs and people. Socialization means training your dog to meet and get along with unfamiliar dogs and people. The only way to accomplish this is for your dog to continue meeting unfamiliar people and dogs daily. Praise your dog and offer a piece of kibble every time he meets an unfamiliar dog or person.

And don't forget to maintain your own improved social life by inviting your friends over at least once a week, just to keep them still involved in training your dog. Ask them to bring along somebody new to meet your dog.

Host a puppy party and invite your dog's buddies from puppy class and the dog park. To offset some of the scarier aspects of the dog world at large — adult dogs, big dogs, and occasionally unfriendly dogs — make sure your adolescent dog has regular opportunity to socialize and play with his core companions.

THE DOG WALK

As soon as it is safe for your puppy to go out, take it on walks — lots of them. There is no better overall socialization exercise and no better overall training exercise. As an added benefit, dog walks are good for *your* health, heart, and soul. Walk that dog! Tie a pink bow to his collar and see how many smiles you get and how many new friends you make. Doggy socialization is good for your social life.

A walk with your dog is the very best socialization and training exercise, and it is the very best exercise for you.

HOUSETRAINING ON WALKS

If you do not have a private yard or garden, make sure your dog urinates and defecates *before* you begin your walk. Thus, the walk becomes a reward for doing the right thing in the right place at the right time. Otherwise, when you terminate an enjoyable walk after your dog has done her duty, you end up punishing her for eliminating. Your dog might then start delaying elimination to prolong her walks.

Don't be forced to use vegetation or deposit slips from your checkbook.

Remember to rubber-band an extra plastic bag to your dog's leash.

Put your puppy on-leash, leave the house, and then stand still and let the pup circle and sniff. Give her three minutes. If she doesn't perform, go back indoors and try again later. Keep your pup in her short-term confinement area for the interim. If your puppy does go within the allotted time, praise her profusely, reward her with a dog treat, say, "Walkies," and off you go. You'll find a simple "no feces = no walk" policy quickly produces a speedy defecator.

Make sure your puppy eliminates in your yard or right outside your front door before setting off for a walk. A walk is the very best reward for a speedy defecator.

There are additional benefits to teaching your dog to eliminate prior to a walk. Clearing up the mess and depositing it in your own trash is much more convenient than a midwalk cleanup. Walking an empty dog empty-handed is also generally more relaxing than walking a dog and lugging around a bag of dog doo.

SOCIALIZING ON WALKS

Take a few time-outs on each walk. Do not rush your young dog through the environment. Give your dog ample opportunity to relax and watch the world go by. A stuffed Kong will help her settle down quickly and calmly each time you stop.

Stop several times during the walk to settle down and read the newspaper while your dog practices settling down and watching the world go by.

Never take your dog's even temperament for granted. The great outdoors can be a scary place, and there will be the occasional surprise to spook your pooch. The best approach is to prevent these problems. Handfeeding your dog his dinner on walks helps him form positive associations with people, other dogs, and traffic. Offer your dog a piece of kibble every time a car, big truck, or noisy motorcycle goes by. Offer your dog a couple of pieces of kibble every time another dog or person passes. Praise your dog and offer a treat whenever he greets another dog or person in a friendly fashion. Praise your dog and offer three tasty treats whenever a child approaches. And when a child whizzes by on a skateboard or dirt bike, handfeed your dog the whole bag of food.

Should someone wish to meet your dog, first show them how to use kibble to lure/reward him to come and sit. Ask the stranger to offer the kibble only after your dog sits to say hello. From the outset, teach your dog to always sit when meeting and greeting people.

TRAINING ON WALKS

When your dog is five months old, puppyhood is over, and you will begin to realize that the canine weight-pulling record approximates ten thousand pounds. Dogs pull on leash for many reasons. The view is always better for the lead dog. A tight leash provides the dog a "telegraph wire" that communicates the owner's intentions, thus affording the dog the luxury of looking around and otherwise checking out the action. Pulling while on-leash appears to be intrinsically enjoyable for dogs. And we let them do it. Each second the leash is tight, each pulling moment is hugely reinforced by each step the dog takes, forging ahead to investigate the ever-exciting, ever-changing olfactory environment.

Here are a few dos and don'ts on teaching your dog to walk calmly on-leash:

DO practice leash-walking around your house and yard from the very beginning and take your puppy for walks in public as soon as he is old enough.

DON'T wait until your dog reaches adolescence before trying to teach him to walk on-leash in public, unless you wish to provide amusement for onlookers.

DO alternate short periods of fifteen to thirty seconds, when your dog walks by your side, with longer periods of a minute or so, when your dog is allowed to range and sniff at the end of the leash. This motivates your dog to walk by your side, as walking side by side is regularly reinforced by permission to range and sniff.

DON'T expect your adolescent (or adult) dog to endlessly heel. He will learn that heeling is mutually exclusive to ranging and sniffing. He won't want to heel and will grow to resent training and the trainer for spoiling his fun.

DO consider training your dog to pull on-leash. Thus, instead of being a problem, pulling on-leash can be the solution, an effective reward to reinforce calmly walking by your side. Alternating slack-leash walking and pulling on-leash is enthusiastically endorsed by my malamutes. Two paws up! Also, on-command leash-pulling is wonderful for ascending steep hills, pulling sleds, soapbox cars, and skateboards.

DON'T allow your dog to decide *when* to pull on-leash. Employ red light/green light training. When your dog tightens the leash, immediately stop, stand still, and wait. Once he slackens the leash, or better yet, once he sits, proceed with the walk.

RED LIGHT / GREEN LIGHT

The good old dog walk has to be one of the dog's biggest rewards, second only to a romp in the park. Many dogs go quite crazy at the prospect of a walk, and, of course, the walk only reinforces their craziness. Moreover, dogs pull on-leash with increasing vigor with every step you take, and, of course, each step you take reinforces the dog's pulling. Luckily, there's a better way. The walk can reinforce your dog's good manners.

Before going on a walk, practice leaving the house in a mannerly fashion. Say, "Walky, Walky, Walkies!" and waggle the dog's leash in front of its nose. Most dogs will go ballistic. Stand still and wait for your dog to calm down and sit. With his walk stalled before starting, your dog will suspect you want him to do something, but as yet he isn't sure what. He will likely offer many creative suggestions, maybe his entire behavior repertoire. Your dog may frantically bark, beg, jump up, lie down, roll over, paw you, and circle you. Ignore everything your dog does until he sits. It doesn't matter how long it takes; your dog will sit eventually. When he does, say, "Good Dog," and snap on his leash. When you do, your dog will likely reactivate. So stand still and wait for him to sit again. When he does, say, "Good Dog," take one step toward the door, stand still, and then wait for him to sit once more. Head toward the door one step at a time and wait for your dog to sit after each step. Have your dog sit before you open the door and have him sit immediately after going through the door. Then come back inside, take off the dog's leash, sit down, and repeat the above procedure.

AVOID UNINTENTIONALLY ENERGIZING YOUR DOG

If your dog explodes with energy after you take only one step, just think how you must be fueling him with energy if you continue walking when he is pulling on-leash. Start by taking just one step at a time and then wait for the dog to calm down and sit before proceeding with the next step. Obviously, you cannot train your dog this way and still get somewhere in a hurry, so take relaxed walks with the specific intention of teaching your dog to walk calmly on-leash.

You'll find that the time it takes for your dog to sit progressively decreases as the exercise proceeds. You'll also notice your dog becomes calmer each time you leave the house. By the third or fourth time you leave, your dog will walk calmly and sit promptly.

Don't prompt your dog to sit. Don't give him any clues. Let

your dog work it out for himself. Your dog is learning even when he presents a series of unwanted behaviors. He is learning what you don't want him to do. The longer you wait for your dog to sit, the better he learns which behaviors are unwanted. When your dog sits and receives praise and a reward, he is learning what you want him to do.

Dogs love this game. After playing the game for a very short time, your dog learns which green-light behaviors (sitting) get you to proceed and which red-light behaviors (everything else) cause you to stand still.

When your dog can leave the house in a mannerly fashion, it is time to go for a real walk. Put your dog's dinner kibble in a bag, for today he will dine on the walk. Hold a piece of kibble in your hand, stand still, and wait for your dog to sit. When he does, say, "Good Dog," and offer the kibble. Then take a giant step forward, stand still, and wait for your dog to sit again. As soon as you step forward, likely your dog will explode with energy. Stand still and wait. Eventually your dog will sit again. Say, "Good Dog," offer the kibble, and take another giant step forward. As you repeat this procedure over and over, you'll notice your dog sits progressively more quickly each time you stand still. After just a few repetitions your dog will begin to sit immediately each time you stop. Now take two giant steps before your stop. Then try three steps and stop, and then five, eight, ten, twenty, and so on. By now you will have discovered that your dog walks calmly and attentively by your side and sits immediately and automatically each time you stop. You will have taught him all this in just one session, and the only words you said were "Good Dog."

SIT AND SETTLE DOWN

Have numerous short training interludes during the walk. Stop for a short training interlude every twenty-five yards or so. For example, each time you stop, say, "Sit," and as soon as your dog sits,

A stuffed Kong may be used as a lure to teach your dog to sit or lie down, and as a source of doggy entertainment while you enjoy the newspaper.

say, "Let's Go," and start walking again. Thus, every time you stop, resuming the walk effectively rewards your dog for sitting.

Keep most training interludes shorter than five seconds, so as to reinforce quick sits and downs or short sequences of body-position changes, such as sit-down-sit-stand-down-stand. You may periodically reward your dog with kibble if you like, but this is hardly necessary, because resuming the walk is a much better treat for your dog. Occasionally insert longer training interludes to practice having your dog walk by your side for fifteen to thirty seconds at a time or to reinforce two- or three-minute settle-downs. Offer a stuffed Kong for your dog's amusement and read a newspaper for yours.

The above training techniques will mold your dog's behavior and mend her manners in a single walk. By averaging seventy or so training sessions per mile, a single walk will troubleshoot virtually any training problem. For example, you may experience some difficulty getting your excited dog to pay attention and settle down the first few times you stop, but by the fourth or fifth time, it will be easy. After an enjoyable three-mile walk (with two hundred or so training interludes), your dog will be nothing less than brilliant.

There are two reasons why this technique is extraordinarily successful:

1. Repeated training interludes force you to face your foremost fears and conquer them. The troubleshooting nature of these repetitive training interludes allows you to solve pressing training problems quickly. For example, your problem is not that your dog does not settle down; it does, but only eventually, only occasionally, and only of her own volition. You want your dog to settle down promptly and reliably upon request. Practice over and over in the above fashion, with many short training interludes during the walk. Your dog will comply more and more quickly with each trial. Eventually, she will learn to comply immediately.

2. Most owners train their dog only in one or two loca-
    tions, such as the kitchen and training class, and they
    end up with a good kitchen dog and a mannerly class
    dog. But the dog still doesn't pay attention on walks
    and in parks. Presumably, the dog thinks that "Sit" only
    means sit in the kitchen and in class, because they are
    the only two places where she has been trained. With
    seventy or so training interludes per mile, however,
    every single practice session is in a different setting
    with different distractions — on quiet streets and busy
    sidewalks, leafy trails and open fields, near schools, and
    in park playgrounds. Thus, your dog learns to heed
    your instructions and quickly and happily comply no
    matter where she is, what she is doing, and what is
    going on. Your dog generalizes the "Sit" command to
    mean sit everywhere and at any time.

If you train your dog on every walk, you will soon have a
puppy that will sit quickly and settle down promptly with a single
request, no matter how excited or distracted she may be. Moreover, your dog settles down willingly and happily because she
knows that being told to lie down is not the end of the world and
not even the end of the walk. Your dog will have learned that
"Settle Down," for example, is just a relaxing time-out with gentle
praise before her exciting life as Walking Dog resumes.

With your now-mannerly dog, you'll find that it is quicker
navigating country roads and suburban sidewalks than with your
previously hyperactive hound. Now you can follow your intended
itinerary without being pulled every which way but loose.

TRAINING IN THE CAR

Don't forget to practice in the car. It's the same technique as on
the walk. For a couple of days, read the newspaper in the car,

having instructed your dog to settle down with a stuffed Kong. Have a short training interlude every minute or so to practice some body-position changes — sit, down, stand, etc. — or place changes — back seat, front seat, seat belt, crate, etc. (For ease and safety, only do this when you are not driving and the car is stationary.) Once your dog promptly responds to each request, repeat the exercises with a friend driving. You'll soon find your dog happily responds to your requests when you are driving.

Make sure you teach your puppy to sit and settle down, and to speak and shush in your stationary car before you drive anywhere. Remember, teaching "Speak" facilitates teaching "Shush."

Once you have a dog who will settle down anytime, anywhere — in the car and on walks — it's time to get him out and about. Be sure to take a bag of kibble with you. Take your dog everywhere — on errands around town, to the bank, pet store, Granny's, to visit friends, to explore the neighborhood, or maybe just for the ride. It's time for picnics in the park, walks, and more walks. And again, always have kibble on hand to give to your dog whenever dogs or people approach. Also, give kibble to strangers to train your dog how to greet them — that is, to sit for a food reward.

TRAINING IN THE DOG PARK

Letting your dog play in the park can be one of the quickest ways to lose control over your adolescent dog. Allow it to play uninterrupted and you'll quickly lose its attention and have no control over it whatsoever. On the other hand, if you integrate training and play, you'll soon develop reliable, off-leash distance control over your dog.

HOW TO TRAIN YOUR DOG NOT TO COME WHEN CALLED

Many owners let their dogs off-leash without so much as a "please" or a sit. Often the dogs are excitedly bouncing and barking in anticipation of playing. Thus being let off-leash reinforces their boisterous behavior. They delight in their newfound freedom, running around, sniffing, chasing each other, and playing together like crazy. The owners look on and chat. Eventually, it's time to go. One owner calls her dog, the dog comes running, the owner snaps on the leash, and the play session is over.

This sequence of events is likely to happen just once or twice, because on subsequent trips to the park the dog understandably will not be quite so keen to come to his owner when called. It doesn't take much for the dog to make the association between coming when called and having an otherwise utterly enjoyable romp in the park abruptly terminated. On future trips to the park, the dog approaches his owner slowly with head down. The owner is now doing a fine job demotivating the dog's recall and is inadvertently training the dog not to come when called.

Indeed, slow recalls quickly become no recalls, as the dog tries to prolong his fun by playing Catch-Me-If-You-Can. The irritated owner now screams for the dog to come, "Bad Dog! Come Here!" And, of course, the dog muses, "I don't think so! In the past I have learned that that nasty tone and volume mean you're not too happy. I think it would be a mite foolish for me to approach you right now. You're not in the best frame of mind to praise and reward me appropriately." But you are not going to do this with your dog, are you?

HOW TO TRAIN YOUR DOG
TO COME WHEN CALLED

Instead, you are going to take your dog's dinner kibble to the park, call your dog every minute or so throughout her play session, have her sit for a couple of pieces of kibble, and then let her go play again. Your dog will soon learn that coming when called is an enjoyable time-out, a little refreshment, a kind word, and a hug from you before she resumes play. Your dog becomes confident that coming when called does not signal the end of the play session. Your dog's enthusiastic recalls will be the talk of the town! When it is time to end the off-leash play session, I like to soften the blow by telling my dogs, "Let's go and find your Kongs!" Before going to the park, I always leave stuffed Kongs in the car and back home as a special treat.

In addition, you might consider teaching your dog an emergency sit or down, which is often better than an emergency recall. Teaching a reliable sit or down is much easier than maintaining a reliable recall. With a quick sit you instantly control your dog's behavior and limit her movement. Once your dog is sitting, you have several options:

1. You may let the dog resume playing. (Either you were just practicing the emergency sit, or the danger has passed.)

2. You may call your dog to you. (The surroundings are changing and it would be safer if your dog were closer; other dogs, people, or especially children are approaching.) Your dog is more likely to come when called if she is already sitting and looking at you, that is, if she is already demonstrating willing compliance.

3. You may instruct your dog to lie down and stay. (The setting is likely to be unstable for a while and it would be safer if your dog were not running around or

running toward you. For example, a group of school-children may be passing between you and your distant dog. To call your dog now would scatter the children like bowling pins.)

4. Walk up to your dog and put her on-leash. For added stability, it is good practice to hold your dog's attention with your hand in a policeman stop signal and continually praise your dog for staying as you approach. (Do this when danger is imminent and a recall or distant stay would be unwise. For example, a herd of one hundred goats is being driven toward your dog. This once happened to my malamute in Tilden Park in Berkeley.)

FOUR STEPS TO AN EMERGENCY DISTANCE SIT

The secret to off-leash control is to thoroughly integrate fun training into all of your dog's off-leash activities. Total integration of training and play should be your aim from the very start. Interrupt your dog's off-leash activities every minute or so. Every time you interrupt an enjoyable activity by instructing your dog to sit, for example, and then allow him to resume the activity, you are reinforcing the dog's prompt sit with a powerful reward. The more you interrupt your dog's play, the more you may reward him for sitting promptly.

First practice the following exercises in safe, enclosed areas. This can be when your puppy is off-leash in your house or yard, when he is playing in puppy classes, during puppy parties, or when off-leash in dog parks.

1. Every minute or so, run up to your puppy and take him by the collar. Praise the pup, offer a tasty food treat, and then tell him to go play again. At first try this

in a fairly small area, such as your kitchen with no other distractions. Then try it with just one other puppy present. If you have difficulty catching your pup, have the other owner grab hers at the same time. Then try with a couple of other puppies present. Gradually increase the number of puppies and size of the area until your puppy is easy to catch when playing, for example, in your fenced yard. Use freeze-dried liver treats during this first exercise so your pup quickly comes to love having his collar grabbed.

2. Once your puppy is easy to catch, dry kibble will suffice. Now, instruct your puppy to sit each time after you take him by the collar. Use the food to lure the puppy into a sitting position, praise the pup as soon as he sits, offer the piece of kibble as reward, and then tell him to go play.

3. By now your puppy should feel completely at ease with your running up to reach for his collar. In fact, he probably looks forward to it, knowing he will receive a food reward before resuming play. You may find your puppy sits in anticipation of the food reward. This is good, because the next step is to instruct your puppy to sit before you reach for his collar. Run up to your puppy, say "Sit," and waggle a piece of kibble under his nose, and once the puppy homes in on the food, use it as a lure to entice him to sit. Praise your puppy as soon as he sits, offer the kibble as reward, and tell the puppy to go play.

It is vital that you do not touch the puppy before he sits. Some owners are impatient and physically sit the dog down. If you have to rely on physical contact to get your dog to sit, you'll never have reliable off-leash control. If you are experiencing difficulties, go back to using freeze-dried liver.

4. Now that your puppy sits promptly as you approach, you can teach him to sit from a distance. Again try this exercise around the house without distractions before trying it with other puppies present. Sit in a chair and without moving a muscle, calmly and quietly say, "Puppy, Sit." Wait a second, then rush toward the puppy saying, "Sit! Sit! Sit!" in an urgent tone but without shouting. Praise your puppy the moment he sits, take him by the collar, offer the piece of kibble as reward, and then let him resume playing. As you repeat this over and over again, you'll discover that fewer and fewer repetitions of the instruction to sit are necessary before your puppy complies. Also, with repeated trials your puppy sits sooner and sooner and with you farther and farther away. Eventually your dog will sit promptly at a single softly spoken request from a distance.

From now on, whenever your dog is off-leash, repeatedly and frequently interrupt his activity with numerous short training interludes. Ninety percent of the training interludes should be as short as one second. Tell your dog to sit and then immediately say, "Go play." Your dog's quick sit is proof that you have control, so you needn't push it. You needn't prolong the sit stay. Instead, quickly tell your dog to go play so as to reinforce the quick sit. In one out of ten training interludes practice something a little different. Once your dog sits, instruct him to sit-stay or to down-stay. Or walk up to your dog and take him by the collar before telling him to resume playing.

INTEGRATE TRAINING AND GAMES

Playing games with lots of rules is a fun way to train your dog and exercise his mind. Your puppy will learn that games have rules and that rules are fun. Training becomes a game, and games become training.

Three visiting Rocky Mountain Search and Rescue shepherds challenge Oso to a home game of cookie-search in the living room.

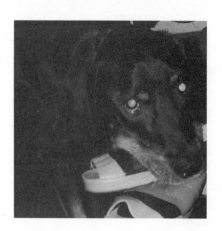

Ivan could search and rescue shoes from any hiding place.

INTEGRATE TRAINING AND LIFESTYLE

In order to get your puppy to respond here, there, and everywhere, he needs be trained here, there, and everywhere. Train your puppy little but often in at least fifty training sessions a day, with only one or two being more than a few seconds long. The secret is to totally integrate training into both your puppy's lifestyle and your lifestyle.

Ivan and Oliver were taught to play a complicated game of tug-o'-war with a rope hanging from the buckeye tree at the bottom of the garden. If you don't teach your dogs how to play games, they will make up their own doggy games with their own doggy rules.

A famous author's dogs enjoy their own version of Keepaway Kong on my couch while their owner researches a book about dogs who never lie.

YOUR PUPPY'S LIFESTYLE

Integrate short training interludes (quick sits and releases) into your puppy's walks and off-leash play. Each quick sit is immediately reinforced by allowing the dog to resume walking or playing — the very best rewards in domestic dogdom. Integrate short training interludes into every enjoyable doggy activity — riding in the car, watching you fix their dinner, lying on the couch, and playing doggy games. For example, have your dog sit before you throw a tennis ball and before you take it back. Progressively increase the length of sit-stay with each repetition.

Similarly, insert short training preludes before all your puppy's enjoyable activities. For example, ask the pup to lie down and roll over for a tummy rub, or to lie down and stay awhile before being invited for a snuggle on the couch. Have her sit before you put her on-leash, before you open the door, before you tell her to jump in the car, before you allow her to get out of the car, and before you let her off-leash. And be sure to have her sit for her supper.

With total integration, your puppy will see no difference between playing and training. Fun times will have structure, and training will be fun!

TV TRAINING

Watching television offers a wonderful training opportunity. Put your puppy's bed plus a couple of stuffed Kongs in front of the television. During the program it is easy to keep an eye on your puppy as he settles down, and commercial breaks are an ideal time for short training interludes. Alternatively, have your puppy settle down while you watch dog-training videos and then periodically let your pup join in as you practice together.

INTEGRATE TRAINING INTO YOUR OWN LIFESTYLE

Train regularly and you'll discover that integrated training is easy and enjoyable. For example, call your puppy for a body-position sequence with variable length stays in each position every time you open the fridge, make a cup of tea, turn a page of the newspaper, or send an e-mail. If you instruct the pup to perform a simple body-position sequence on every such occasion, you will easily be able to train your puppy over fifty times a day without deviating from your normal lifestyle. Remember that you are responsible for a young, impressionable, developing canine brain. Exercise that doggy brain. Allow your pup to achieve and enjoy his full potential.

Oso practices a sit-stay in the hammock prior to moving on to the settle-down exercise.

Once your dog is well-trained, he may enjoy full run of your house, will be welcome almost anywhere, and may eventually graduate to couch work. My dogs spend most of the time snuggled on the couch. They like the Discovery Channel. Occasionally, I may ask them to do something during breaks, like move over, fetch the paper, change the channel, vacuum the living room, or fix dinner. They're highly trained dogs.

Phoenix was always a natural at couch work.

CHAPTER NINE

Puppy Priorities

For quick reference, I've summarized the main points of this book — your puppy priorities — listed in order of urgency and ranked in terms of importance.

1. Household Etiquette — From the very first day your puppy comes home

Housetraining, chewtoy-training, and teaching your dog alternatives to recreational barking are by far the most pressing items on your puppy's educational agenda. From day one, employ errorless management teaching programs, comprising confinement schedules plus the liberal use of chewtoys (Kongs, Biscuit Balls, and sterilized long bones) stuffed with kibble. Simple behavior problems are so easily preventable, yet they are the most common reasons for people's dissatisfaction with their dogs and the most common reasons for dog euthanasia. Teaching household manners should be your number one priority the first day your puppy comes home.

#1 Urgency Rating: Household etiquette is by far the most pressing item on your new puppy's educational agenda. If you want to avoid annoying behavior problems, training must begin the very first day your puppy comes home.

#3 Importance Rating: Teaching household etiquette is extremely important. Puppies quickly become unwelcome when their owners allow them to develop housesoiling, chewing, barking, digging, and escaping problems.

2. Home Alone — During the first few days and weeks your puppy is at home

Sadly, the maddening pace of present-day domestic dogdom necessitates teaching your puppy how to enjoy spending time at home alone — not only to ensure your pup adheres to established household etiquette when unsupervised, but more importantly to prevent your puppy from becoming anxious in your absence. Normally, these go hand in hand; for when puppies become anxious they tend to bark, chew, dig, and urinate more frequently. From the outset, and especially during its first few days and weeks in your home, your puppy needs to be taught how to entertain himself quietly, calmly, and confidently. Otherwise he most certainly will become severely stressed when left at home alone.

#2 Urgency Rating: Teaching your pup to confidently enjoy his own company is the second most urgent item on his educational agenda. It would be unfair to smother the puppy with attention and affection during his first days or weeks at home, only to subject the pup to solitary confinement when the adults go back to work and children go back to school. During the first few days and weeks when you are around to monitor your puppy's behavior, teach him to enjoy quiet moments confined to his puppy playroom or doggy den. Especially be sure to provide some form of occupational therapy (stuffed chewtoys) for your puppy to busy himself and enjoyably pass the time while you are away.

#3 Importance Rating: Preparing your puppy for time alone is extremely important both for your peace of mind — to prevent housesoiling, chewing, and barking problems — and especially for your puppy's peace of mind. It is absolutely no fun for a pup to be overdependent, stressed, and anxious.

3. Socialization with People — Always, but especially before twelve weeks of age

Many puppy-training techniques focus on teaching your puppy to enjoy the company and actions of people. Well-socialized dogs are confident and friendly, rather than fearful and aggressive. Show all family members, visitors, and strangers how to get your puppy to come, sit, lie down, roll over, and enjoy being handled for pieces of kibble. Living with an undersocialized dog can be frustrating, difficult, and potentially dangerous. For undersocialized dogs, life is also unbearably stressful.

#3 Urgency Rating: Many people think that puppy classes are for socializing puppies with people. This is not strictly true. Certainly puppy classes provide a convenient venue for socialized puppies to continue socializing with people. However, puppies must be well socialized toward people before they attend classes at twelve weeks of age. The time window for socialization closes at three months of age, and so there is some urgency to adequately socialize your puppy to people. During your pup's first month at home, he needs to meet and interact positively with at least one hundred different people!

#2 Importance Rating: Socializing your puppy to enjoy people is vital — second only in importance to your pup learning to inhibit the force of his bite and develop a soft mouth. Socialization must never end. Remember, your adolescent dog will begin to desocialize unless he continues to meet unfamiliar people every day. Walk your dog or expand your own social life at home.

4. Dog-Dog Socialization — Between three months and eighteen weeks

As soon as your puppy turns three months old, it is time to play catch-up with dog-dog socialization. It's time for puppy classes, long walks, and visits to dog parks. Well-socialized dogs would rather play than bite or fight. And well-socialized dogs usually bite more gently, if ever they should bite or fight.

#4 Urgency Rating: If you would like to have an adult dog who enjoys the company of other dogs, puppy classes and walks are essential, especially since many puppies have been sequestered indoors until they have been immunized against parvovirus and other serious doggy diseases — by the very earliest at three months of age.

#6 Importance Rating: It is hard to rate the importance of dog-dog socialization. Depending on the lifestyle of the owners, dog-friendliness may be either unnecessary or essential. If you would like to enjoy walks with your adult dog, early socialization in puppy classes and dog parks is essential. Surprisingly, though, very few people walk their dogs. Whereas large dogs and urban dogs tend to be walked quite frequently, small dogs and suburban dogs are seldom walked.

Regardless of the desired sociability of your adult dog, dog-dog play and especially play-fighting and play-biting during puppyhood are absolutely essential for the development of bite inhibition and a soft mouth. For this reason alone, puppy classes and trips to the dog park are the top priority at three months of age.

5. Sit and Settle Down Commands — Begin anytime you would like your puppy dog to listen to you

If you teach your dog just a couple of commands, they would have to be "Sit" and "Settle Down." Just think of all the mischievous things your puppy dog cannot do when she is sitting.

#5 Urgency Rating: Unlike socialization and bite inhibition, which must occur during puppyhood, you may teach your dog to sit and settle down at any age, so there is no great urgency. Because it is so easy and so much fun to teach young puppies, however, why not start teaching basic manners the very first day you bring your puppy home — or as early as four or five weeks if you are raising the litter? The only urgency to teach these simple and effective control commands would be if ever your puppy's antics or activity level begin to irritate you. Sit or Settle Down will solve most problems.

#5 Importance Rating: It is difficult to rate the importance of basic manners. Personally I like dogs who can enjoy being dogs without being a bother to other people. On the other hand, many people happily live with dogs without any formal training whatsoever. If you consider your dog to be perfect for you, make your own choice. But if you or other people find your dog's behavior to be annoying, why not teach him how to behave? Indeed, a simple sit prevents the majority of annoying behavior problems, including jumping up, dashing through doorways, running away, bothering people, chasing its tail, chasing the cat, etc. The list is long! It is so much easier to teach your dog how to act from the outset by teaching the one right way — sitting — rather than trying to correct the many things he does wrong. Regardless, it would be unfair to get on your dog's case for bad manners if he is only breaking rules he didn't know existed.

6. Bite Inhibition — By eighteen weeks of age

A soft mouth is the single most important quality for any dog. Hopefully, your dog will never bite or fight, but if he does, well-established bite inhibition ensures that your dog causes little if any damage.

Socialization is an ongoing process of ever-widening experience and confidence building that helps your pup to comfortably handle the challenges and changes of everyday adult life. It is impossible to prepare your puppy for every possible eventuality, however, and on those rare occasions when adult dogs are badly hurt, frightened, scared, or upset, they seldom write letters of complaint. Instead, dogs customarily growl and bite, so the level of bite inhibition training from puppyhood predetermines the seriousness of the damage.

Adult dogs with poor bite inhibition rarely mouth and seldom bite, but when they do, the bites almost always break the skin. Adult dogs with well-established bite inhibition often mouth during play, and should they bite, the bites almost never break the skin because during puppyhood the dog learned how to register a complaint without inflicting any damage.

Bite inhibition is one of the most misunderstood aspects of behavioral development in dogs (and other animals). Many owners make the catastrophic mistake of stopping their puppy from mouthing altogether. If a puppy is not allowed to play-bite, she cannot develop reliable bite inhibition. Pups are born virtual biting machines with needle sharp teeth so that they learn biting hurts before they develop the jaw strength to cause appreciable harm. However, they cannot learn to inhibit the force of their bites if they are never allowed to play-bite and play-fight.

Bite inhibition training comprises first teaching the puppy to progressively inhibit the force of its bites until painful puppy play-biting is toned down and transformed into gentle puppy mouthing, and then, and only then, teaching her to progressively inhibit the incidence of her mouthing. Thus the puppy learns that mouthing is by and large inappropriate and that any pressured bite is absolutely unacceptable.

#6 Urgency Rating: You have until your puppy is four and a half months old, so take your time to ensure your puppy masters this most important item in its educational curriculum. The more your puppy bites, the safer its jaws will be as an adult, since she has had more opportunities to learn that biting hurts.

If you are worried about your puppy's biting behavior, enroll in a puppy class immediately. You may seek further advice from the trainer, and your puppy may let off steam and redirect many of her bites toward other puppies during play sessions.

#1 Importance Rating: Bite inhibition is of crucial importance, by far the single most important quality of any dog, or any animal. Living with a dog who does not have reliable bite inhibition is unpleasant and dangerous. And bite inhibition must be acquired during puppyhood. You must fully understand how to teach your puppy. Attempting to teach bite inhibition to an adolescent or adult dog is often extremely difficult, dangerous, and time-consuming.

THE MOST IMPORTANT THINGS TO TEACH YOUR PUPPY

1. Bite Inhibition
2. Socialization with People
3. Household Etiquette
3. Home Alone
5. Sit and Settle Down Commands
6. Dog–Dog Socialization

THE MOST URGENT THINGS TO TEACH YOUR PUPPY

1. Household Etiquette
2. Home Alone
3. Socialization with People
4. Dog–Dog Socialization
5. Sit and Settle Down Commands
6. Bite Inhibition

CHAPTER TEN

Homework Schedules

All behavior, training, and temperament problems are easy to prevent in puppyhood. The same problems can be time-consuming and extremely difficult to resolve in adulthood. Separation anxiety, fearfulness, and aggression toward people must be prevented before your puppy is three months old. Consequently, have family members and friends check that you do your homework each day. Your puppy can't learn if you don't teach him.

Photocopy (and enlarge) the homework schedule for each week. Check each box or include a score (number of times, length of time, percentage) where appropriate.

HOME ALONE IN THE HOUSEHOLD

During its first week in your home, your puppy must learn house-training and household manners, and how to amuse himself when left by himself. Success depends on two things: (1) your puppy spending most of his time in the self-teaching environments of short-term and long-term confinement and (2) your puppy receiving all of his food from stuffed chewtoys or being handfed by people vs. food quickly gobbled down "for free" from a bowl.

Percentage of time your puppy spends in:

	S	S	M	T	W	T	F
Short-term confinement with stuffed chewtoys............................	❏	❏	❏	❏	❏	❏	❏
Long-term confinement with stuffed chewtoys and a toilet...........	❏	❏	❏	❏	❏	❏	❏
Playing and training with people with 100% supervision and feedback..............	❏	❏	❏	❏	❏	❏	❏
Investigating the house with 100% supervision and feedback..............	❏	❏	❏	❏	❏	❏	❏
Investigating the house or yard with no supervision................................	❏	❏	❏	❏	❏	❏	❏

Remember, with unsupervised free range of your house or yard, your puppy will develop a predictable series of problems: house-soiling, chewing, barking, digging, escaping, and other anxiety-induced problems.

Percentage of your pup's daily diet (kibble and treats) that he received in:

Hollow chewtoys..................................	❏	❏	❏	❏	❏	❏	❏
Handfed as rewards by strangers..............	❏	❏	❏	❏	❏	❏	❏
Handfed as rewards by family and friends...	❏	❏	❏	❏	❏	❏	❏

Percentage of time you practiced:

Long-term confinement when at home..	❏	❏	❏	❏	❏	❏	❏

Short-term confinement in   S   S   M   T   W   T   F
different rooms.....................................❑   ❑   ❑   ❑   ❑   ❑   ❑

Occasionally, put your puppy in its long-term confinement area when you are home to monitor her behavior. As soon as your puppy has learned to settle down quickly and quietly with a chewtoy, you will be able to dispense with the crate for short-term confinement.

Number of food rewards that your
puppy received for using her toilet area...❑   ❑   ❑   ❑   ❑   ❑   ❑

Note: This is the quickest way to housetrain your puppy!

Number of times your puppy
ate from her food bowl...........................❑   ❑   ❑   ❑   ❑   ❑   ❑

Note: Unless you are practicing food bowl exercises (see pages 131–133), you are wasting precious kibble for stuffing chewtoys and for family, friends, and strangers to use as rewards when training the puppy.

Number of chewing mistakes.................❑   ❑   ❑   ❑   ❑   ❑   ❑
Number of housesoiling mishaps............❑   ❑   ❑   ❑   ❑   ❑   ❑

During your puppy's first few weeks at home, any mistake should be viewed seriously. Puppies with housesoiling and chewing problems are usually relegated and confined to the yard, where they bark, dig, and escape out of boredom and anxiety. Early confinement with stuffed chewtoys teaches your puppy what to chew, when and where to eliminate, and to settle down quietly. Keeping your well-behaved puppy indoors prevents him from digging or escaping.

BITE INHIBITION

Number of play-mouthing   S   S   M   T   W   T   F
and play-fighting sessions......................❑   ❑   ❑   ❑   ❑   ❑   ❑

The more you provide appropriate feedback to your puppy when he mouths and bites your hands, the more quickly he will learn to decrease the force of his bites, and the safer his jaws will be in adulthood. The number of times your puppy bites or mouths you will increase steadily as your pup's stamina and desire to play increase throughout puppyhood and adolescence. However, the number of times your puppy hurts you should peak at three and a half months of age as his jaws become more powerful and then decrease as your puppy learns to be more gentle.

Number of times your puppy's
biting behavior hurt you......................❑   ❑   ❑   ❑   ❑   ❑   ❑

Daily ouches should have decreased significantly by four months of age. If not, seek help from a trainer immediately.

Number of training interludes
(sits or settle-downs) per session.............❑   ❑   ❑   ❑   ❑   ❑   ❑

You cannot interrupt play sessions too many times. Each time you stop playing, resuming play may be used as a reward for stopping.

Number of times you supervised
your puppy's play with
squeaky toys and soft toys.....................❑   ❑   ❑   ❑   ❑   ❑   ❑

The above exercise is essential for toy survival and one of the best ways to teach your puppy to be gentle with its jaws. Remember, stuffed animals and squeaky toys are not chewtoys: their destruction and consumption is extremely dangerous for your dog!

Have you taught your puppy to speak (bark and growl) on cue? Now is the best time to do it.

Have you signed up for puppy class yet? Puppy classes offer the best controlled venue for your puppy to learn bite inhibition.

SOCIALIZATION AND TRAINING AT HOME

Your puppy must socialize with at least one hundred people before she is three months old. That's just twenty-five people a week, or four a day. List the number of people who met your puppy:

	S	S	M	T	W	T	F
Total number of people	❑	❑	❑	❑	❑	❑	❑
Number of men	❑	❑	❑	❑	❑	❑	❑
Number of strangers	❑	❑	❑	❑	❑	❑	❑
Total number of children	❑	❑	❑	❑	❑	❑	❑
Number of babies (0–2 years old)	❑	❑	❑	❑	❑	❑	❑
Number of toddlers (2–4 years old)	❑	❑	❑	❑	❑	❑	❑
Number of children (4–12 years old)	❑	❑	❑	❑	❑	❑	❑
Number of teenagers (13–19 years old)	❑	❑	❑	❑	❑	❑	❑

Supervise puppy and human youngsters at all times. Let the puppy sniff the baby's diapers. Protect the baby's face and hands. Toddlers may handfeed and train the puppy if you enclose their hand in yours. Children and teenagers are the very best puppy trainers if they have proper instruction and supervision.

Number of puppy parties	❑	❑	❑	❑	❑	❑	❑
Number of people at each party	❑	❑	❑	❑	❑	❑	❑
Number of guests who trained your puppy to come, sit, lie down, and stay	❑	❑	❑	❑	❑	❑	❑
Number of funny people at each party	❑	❑	❑	❑	❑	❑	❑

Your puppy needs to be exposed to people wearing hats, helmets, sunglasses, and beards, as well as people acting weird, making funny faces, staring, walking like John Cleese, laughing, giggling, crying, talking loudly, and pretending to argue.

	S	S	M	T	W	T	F
Number of guests who held (hugged/restrained) your puppy.............	❑	❑	❑	❑	❑	❑	❑

Number of guests who offered kibble after examining your puppy's:

Muzzle..	❑	❑	❑	❑	❑	❑	❑
Two ears..	❑	❑	❑	❑	❑	❑	❑
Four paws..	❑	❑	❑	❑	❑	❑	❑
Rear end..	❑	❑	❑	❑	❑	❑	❑

Number of times a family member offered kibble after:

Examining the puppy's muzzle...............	❑	❑	❑	❑	❑	❑	❑
Examining both ears............................	❑	❑	❑	❑	❑	❑	❑
Examining each paw............................	❑	❑	❑	❑	❑	❑	❑
Hugging/restraining the puppy...............	❑	❑	❑	❑	❑	❑	❑
Giving the puppy a tummy rub...............	❑	❑	❑	❑	❑	❑	❑
Taking hold of the puppy's collar............	❑	❑	❑	❑	❑	❑	❑
Grooming the puppy............................	❑	❑	❑	❑	❑	❑	❑
Examining and cleaning the pup's teeth...	❑	❑	❑	❑	❑	❑	❑
Clipping the puppy's nails....................	❑	❑	❑	❑	❑	❑	❑

Number of pieces of kibble handfed when teaching the puppy to come, sit, lie down, and stay...

	❑	❑	❑	❑	❑	❑	❑

Number of pieces of kibble handfed to your puppy when teaching "Off," "Take it," and "Gennnntly".................	S	S	M	T	W	T	F
	❏	❏	❏	❏	❏	❏	❏

Number of toy exchanges (balls, bones, chewtoys, paper tissue) for kibble when teaching the puppy, "Off!", "Take it!" and "Thank you!"................................ ❏ ❏ ❏ ❏ ❏ ❏ ❏

Number of food bowl exercises.............. ❏ ❏ ❏ ❏ ❏ ❏ ❏

SOCIALIZATION AND TRAINING IN THE WORLD AT LARGE

The big wide world can be a scary place for a three-month-old pup. Do not rush your puppy through the environment. Choose a quiet street near your house or apartment and give your puppy all the time in the world to watch the world go by. Make sure you take your puppy's dinner kibble in a picnic bag. After a half dozen or so picnics, your puppy will be unflappable — been there, done that, like that!

- Handfeed your puppy a piece of kibble each time a person or another dog passes by.

- Offer a liver treat each time a child, truck, motorbike, bicycle, or skateboarder whizzes by. Have liver treats for strangers and children to feed to your pup when she sits. Have puppy party guests initially expose your puppy to bicycles, skateboards, and other moving objects. Thus, potentially scary stimuli are much more controllable.

- Repeat the above procedure on a busier street, in a downtown commercial area, near a children's playground, in a shopping center, and in a rural area around other animals. Make sure your puppy gets to spend time exploring office buildings, staircases, elevators, and slippery floors.

	S	S	M	T	W	T	F
Number of unfamiliar people who met your puppy.............................	❏	❏	❏	❏	❏	❏	❏
Number of unfamiliar dogs who met your puppy............................	❏	❏	❏	❏	❏	❏	❏

To remain sociable and friendly, your puppy needs to meet at least three unfamiliar people and three unfamiliar dogs each day. Otherwise, he will desocialize dramatically during adolescence (between four and a half months and two years of age).

Number of walks..................................	❏	❏	❏	❏	❏	❏	❏
Number of trips to the dog park..............	❏	❏	❏	❏	❏	❏	❏
Number of training interludes (sits and downs) per walk.........................	❏	❏	❏	❏	❏	❏	❏
Number of one-minute settle-downs per walk..	❏	❏	❏	❏	❏	❏	❏
Number of recalls or emergency sits and downs in dog park......................	❏	❏	❏	❏	❏	❏	❏
Number of times your puppy peed 'n' pooped prior to a walk..............	❏	❏	❏	❏	❏	❏	❏
Number of times you trained your puppy in the car............................	❏	❏	❏	❏	❏	❏	❏
Number of times you praised and rewarded your puppy after he greeted another dog.............................	❏	❏	❏	❏	❏	❏	❏

List your puppy's top ten favorite activities and games that you use as life rewards to integrate training into your puppy's lifestyle.

1.

2.

3.

4.

5.

6.

7.

8.

9.

10.

List the games you play with your puppy to make training easy and enjoyable. Check out the list of fun books and videos on page 213.

	S	S	M	T	W	T	F
Number of times you were upset by your puppy's behavior.....................	❏	❏	❏	❏	❏	❏	❏
Number of times you reprimanded or punished your puppy.....................	❏	❏	❏	❏	❏	❏	❏

If things are not going as planned and you are dissatisfied with your puppy's progress, seek help from a trainer immediately.

If you have dutifully accomplished everything described in this book, congratulations! You should now enjoy a long life with your good-natured, well-mannered canine companion. Give your dog a special bone today. "Good dog!" And give yourself a resounding pat on the back. "Well done! Goooood owner!"

CHAPTER ELEVEN

Books and Videos

Most bookshops and pet stores offer a bewildering choice of dog books and videos. Consequently a number of dog training associations have voted on what they consider to be the most useful titles for prospective puppy owners. I have included the lists as voted by the Dog Friendly Dog Trainers Group. Also included in parentheses are the ranks of each book and video as voted by the Association of Pet Dog Trainers — the largest association of professional pet dog trainers worldwide — as well as by the Canadian Association of Professional Pet Dog Trainers.

Most of the books and videos are practical puppy-raising guides, primarily comprising useful training tips and techniques. In addition, I have included lists of my own: a list for those of you who especially want to have fun with your dog, and lists for those who are interested in a better understanding of dog behavior and psychology.

TOP FIVE BEST VIDEOS

#1 *Sirius Puppy Training* — Ian Dunbar
James & Kenneth Publishers, 1987. (CAPPDT #1,
APDT #1)

#2 *Training Dogs with Dunbar* — Ian Dunbar
James & Kenneth Publishers, 1996. (CAPPDT #2,
APDT #4)

#3 *Training the Companion Dog* (4 videos) — Ian Dunbar
James & Kenneth Publishers, 1992. (APDT #2, Winner
of the Dog Writers Association of America Maxwell
Award for Best Dog Training Video)

#4 *Dog Training for Children* — Ian Dunbar
James & Kenneth Publishers, 1996.

#5 *Puppy Love: Raise Your Dog the Clicker Way* — Karen
Pryor & Carolyn Clark. Sunshine Books, 1999.

TOP TEN BEST BOOKS

#1 *How to Teach a New Dog Old Tricks* — Ian Dunbar
James & Kenneth Publishers, 1991. (APDT #1,
CAPPDT #4)

#2 *Doctor Dunbar's Good Little Dog Book* — Ian Dunbar
James & Kenneth Publishers, 1992. (APDT #5,
CAPPDT #6)

#3 *The Power of Positive Dog Training* — Pat Miller
Hungry Minds, 2001.

#4 *The Perfect Puppy* — Gwen Bailey
Hamlyn, 1995. (APDT #8)

#5 *Dog Friendly Dog Training* — Andrea Arden
IDG Books Worldwide, 2000.

#6 *Positive Puppy Training Works* — Joel Walton
David & James Publishers, 2002.

#7 *Train Your Dog the Lazy Way* — Andrea Arden
Alpha Books, 1999.

#8 *Behavior Booklets* (9 booklets) — Ian Dunbar
James & Kenneth Publishers, 1985. (APDT #9)

#9 *25 Stupid Mistakes Dog Owners Make* — Janine Adams
Lowell House, 2000.

#10* *The Dog Whisperer* — Paul Owens
Adams Media Corporation, 1999.

BOOKS / VIDEOS FOR DOGGY INTEREST

#1 *The Culture Clash* — Jean Donaldson
James & Kenneth Publishers, 1996. (CAPPDT #1, APDT #2)

#2 *Don't Shoot the Dog* — Karen Pryor
Bantam Books, 1985. (CAPPDT #2, APDT #7)

#3 *Bones Would Rain from the Sky* — Suzanne Clothier
Warner Books, 2002.

#4 *The Other End of the Leash* — Patricia McConnell
Ballantine Books, 2002.

#5 *Dog Behavior* — Ian Dunbar
TFH Publications, 1979. (CAPPDT #6)

#6 *Behavior Problems in Dogs* — William Campbell
Behavior Rx Systems, 1999. (CAPPDT #6)

#7 *Biting & Fighting* (2 videos) — Ian Dunbar
James & Kenneth Publishers, 1994.

#8 *Dog Language* — Roger Abrantes
Wakan Tanka Publishers, 1997.

#9 *Excel-erated Learning: Explaining How Dogs Learn and How Best to Teach Them* — Pamela Reid
James & Kenneth Publishers, 1996.

#10 *How Dogs Learn* — Mary Burch & Jon Bailey
Howell Book House, 1999.

BOOKS / VIDEOS FOR DOGGY FUN

#1 *Take a Bow Wow & Bow Wow Take 2* (2 videos) —
Virginia Broitman & Sherri Lippman,
Take a Bow Wow, 1995. (APDT #5, CAPPDT #7)

#2 *The Trick Is in the Training* — Stephanie Taunton & Cheryl Smith, Barron's, 1998.

#3 *Fun and Games with Your Dog* — Gerd Ludwig
Barron's, 1996.

#4 *Dog Tricks: Step by Step* — Mary Zeigenfuse & Jan Walker, Howell Book House, 1997.

#5 *Fun & Games with Dogs* — Roy Hunter
Howlin Moon Press, 1993.

#6 *Canine Adventures* — Cynthia Miller
Animalia Publishing Company, 1999.

#7 *Getting Started: Clicker Training for Dogs* — Karen Pryor,
Sunshine Books, 2002.

#8 *Clicker Fun* (3 videos) — Deborah Jones
Canine Training Systems, 1996.

#9 *Agility Tricks* — Donna Duford
Clean Run Productions, 1999.

#10 *My Dog Can Do That!*
ID Tag Company. 1991.
The board game you play with your dog

Index

About the Author

One of the world's leading authorities on dog training and behavior, Dr. Ian Dunbar is a veterinarian, animal behaviorist, and writer. The original creator and popularizer of off-leash puppy classes, he has sparked several revolutions in dog training, including the move to positive, reward-based training. He is the founder of many dog-training organizations, including the Center for Applied Animal Behavior; the Association of Pet Dog Trainers, the largest and most influential worldwide association of professional pet dog trainers; and Sirius® Puppy Training, the original and leading provider of puppy training classes in the San Francisco Bay Area (www.siriuspup.com).

Dr. Dunbar received his veterinary degree and a special honors degree in physiology from the Royal Veterinary College in London and his Ph.D. in animal behavior from the University of California at Berkeley, where he spent ten years researching the development of hierarchical social behavior and aggression in domestic dogs. He has given nearly eight hundred full-day seminars and workshops for dog trainers and veterinarians around the world. His ongoing work — including six books, eleven videos, his behavior column in the American Kennel Club *Gazette,* and the television program *Dogs with Dunbar,* which is shown through-out Europe on the Discovery Channel — have won numerous awards. He has been inducted into the prestigious *Dog Fancy* Hall of Fame along with four of his heroes: James Herriot, Konrad Lorenz, Lassie, and Balto. He lives in Berkeley, California, with Kelly — and Claude, Ollie, Dune, Ugly, and Mayhem.

In Memory of
Ivan